STAFFOR
UNIVERSITY

REFERENCE ONLY
NOT TO BE
TAKEN AWAY.

ICT IN THE EARLY YEARS

Learning and Teaching with Information and Communications Technology

Series Editors: Anthony Adams and Sue Brindley

The role of ICT in the curriculum is much more than simply a passing trend. It provides a real opportunity for teachers of all phases and subjects to rethink fundamental pedagogical issues alongside the approaches to learning that pupils need to apply in classrooms. In this way it foregrounds the ways in which teachers can match in school the opportunities for learning provided in the home and community. The series is firmly rooted in practice and also explores the theoretical underpinning of the ways in which curriculum content and skills can be developed by the effective integration of ICT in schooling. It addresses the educational needs of the early years, the primary phase and secondary subject areas. The books are appropriate for pre-service teacher training and continuing professional development as well as for those pursuing higher degrees in education.

Published and forthcoming titles:

Adams and Brindley (eds): *Teaching Secondary English with ICT*
Barton (ed.): *Teaching Secondary Science with ICT*
Florian and Hegarty (eds): *ICT and Special Educational Needs*
Johnston-Wilder and Pimm (eds): *Teaching Secondary Maths with ICT*
Loveless and Dore (eds): *ICT in the Primary School*
Monteith (ed.): *Teaching Primary Literacy with ICT*
Monteith (ed.): *Teaching Secondary School Literacies with ICT*
Way and Beardon (eds): *ICT and Primary Mathematics*
Warwick, Wilson and Winterbottom (eds): *Teaching and Learning Primary Science with ICT*

ICT IN THE EARLY YEARS

Edited by
Mary Hayes and David Whitebread

 Open University Press

Open University Press
McGraw-Hill Education
McGraw-Hill House
Shoppenhangers Road
Maidenhead
Berkshire
England
SL6 2QL

email:enquiries@openup.co.uk
world wide web: www.openup.co.uk

and Two Penn Plaza, New York, NY 10121-2289, USA

First Published 2006

Copyright © Mary Hayes and David Whitebread 2006

All rights reserved. Except for the quotation of short passages for the purpose of criticism and review, no part of this publication may be reproduced, stored in a retrieval system, or transmitted, in any form or by any means, electronic, mechanical, photocopying, recording or otherwise, without the prior written permission of the publisher or a licence from the Copyright Licensing Agency Limited. Details of such licences (for reprographic reproduction) may be obtained from the Copyright Licensing Agency Ltd of 90 Tottenham Court Road, London, W1T 4LP.

A catalogue record of this book is available from the British Library.

ISBN-10: 0335 20808 8 (pb)   0335 20809 6 (hb)
ISBN-13: 978 0335 20808 1 (pb)   978 0335 20809 8 (hb)

Library of Congress Cataloging-in-Publication Data
CIP data applied for

Typeset by RefineCatch Limited, Bungay, Suffolk
Printed in Poland by OZGraf S.A.
www.polskabook.pl

CONTENTS

List of figures and tables   vii
List of contributors   ix
Series editors' preface   xiii

Introduction: Teaching for tomorrow   1
Mary Hayes

1   What do the children have to say?   6
    Mary Hayes

2   ICT: Play and exploration   21
    Carol Fine and Mary Lou Thornbury

3   Literacy and ICT in the early years   37
    Tim Waller

4   Mathematics and ICT in the early years   55
    Richard Bennett

5   Science and ICT in the early years   72
    Rosemary Feasey and Margaret Still

6	Creativity, problem-solving and playful uses of technology: Games and simulations in the early years *David Whitebread*	86
7	Visual literacy and painting with technology: Observations in the early years classroom *Janet Cooke and John Woollard*	107
8	Digital animation in the early years: ICT and media education *Jackie Marsh*	123
9	Using ICT to enhance the learning of music *Mary Hayes, Chris Taylor and David Wheway*	136
10	Towards a future early years: ICT Curriculum *Iram and John Siraj-Blatchford*	153
	Index	163

LIST OF FIGURES AND TABLES

Figures

2.1	Active ICT	27
3.1	Frequency of observed interaction (by type)	49
4.1	Age distribution in the classes taught (n = 41)	65
4.2	Type of program and frequency of use	66
4.3	Frequency of computer based activity	66
6.1	Logo problems from *Crystal Rain Forest*	89
6.2	Adventure game maps	95
6.3	The Witch from *Granny's Garden*	105
8.1	Chloe's storyboard	129
8.2	Stills from Chloe's film	130
9.1	Sequencing illustration	142
9.2	*Super Duper Music Looper*	143
9.3	*The Beat Machine* from Radio 3s *Making tracks* website	143
9.4	Cables from left: large jack, large jack with large to mini jack converter XLR	145
9.5	Standard icons on household recording equipment	145
9.6	Icons indicating presence of a soundcard	147
9.7	Sound Recorder: standard menu icons	148
9.8	Sound Recorder: improving sound quality	149

9.9 A child holds a microphone to record sounds through a drainpipe while the teacher operates a portable mini-disk recorder   150

Tables

1.1	Different types of knowledge and levels of learning in ICT	8
1.2	Planning for ICT and the types of learning involved	17
5.1	The language of science, ICT and everyday: the example of temperature sensors	79
7.1	How pupils use icons	113
8.1	Knowledge, skills and understanding developed in the animation activity	127

LIST OF CONTRIBUTORS

Richard Bennett is a senior lecturer in ICT at the University of Chester. He is ICT Co-ordinator in the School of Education and teaches on BEd, PGCE and CPD courses. He has been a primary school teacher and headteacher, an Ofsted inspector and director of a teachers' centre. He has a particular interest in early years' education, and has a number of recent publications related to both ICT and the Early Years.

Janet Cooke is a consultant and advisory teacher for assessment across the primary age range. She was a primary school teacher with many years of experience. She carried out research at the University of Southampton and in schools across Cambridgeshire.

Rosemary Feasey is a leading expert in primary science. She is currently a freelance consultant working with a range of schools across the UK and working overseas. Rosemary was the first person from a primary science background to become Chair of the Association for Science Education (ASE) in its 100 year history. She is passionate about primary science, has always been proactive in primary science and worked to change the nature of primary science and develop the quality of science education. She regularly works with schools in the north-east of England, teaching a range of pupils from 4-year-olds through to 11-year-olds. She has written a range of publications on a variety of topics.

Carol Fine after great success as an Early Years teacher in North Kensington, Carol embarked on a career in IT during the formative years of the Inner London Educational Computing Centre. She then moved into In-service and Teacher Education at the University of North London, now London Metropolitan. Her final post of principal lecturer at Kingston University was as subject leader for ICT. Sadly Carol died before this book was published. The book is dedicated to her.

Mary Hayes was an early years' teacher for 20 years and successfully integrated computers into a vertically grouped open plan situation in the days when software was loaded from a tape recorder! Her research recently focused on European collaboration through the use of ICT, and research into the use of communications technology with early years' pupils. She is now an education adviser to hospital consultants at Kent Surrey and Sussex Deanery within London University.

Jackie Marsh is Reader in Education at the University of Sheffield where she teaches on early childhood and literacy Masters and EdD programmes. She is an editor of the *Journal of Early Childhood Literacy* (Sage). Jackie is involved in research which examines the role and nature of literacy, both in- and out-of-school contexts, and her most recent work in this area was the 'Digital Beginnings' project, funded by BBC Worldwide and the Esmée Fairbairn Foundation (see the project website at http://www.digitalbeginnings.shef.ac.uk/).

Iram Siraj-Blatchford is currently Professor of Early Childhood Education at the Institute of Education, University of London. She is co-director of the major DfEE study on Effective Provision of Pre-school Education (EPPE) Project (extended as EPPE 3–11 to 2008). She also directed the influential Researching Effective Pedagogy in the Early Years (REPEY) project, and is currently directing a major evaluation of the Foundation Phase in Wales. She has published extensively on equality of opportunity and quality in the early years education. Iram and John Siraj-Blatchford have conducted a number of research projects together.

John Siraj-Blatchford is based in the Faculty of Education, University of Cambridge and is currently serving as an associate director of the ESRC Teaching and Learning Research Programme (TLRP). His publications include *Supporting Information and Communications Technology in the Early Years* (with D. Whitebread, Open University Press 2003) and *Developing New Technologies for Young Children* (Trentham Books 2004), which is an account of the 11 million Euro Experimental School Environments (ESE) initiative from the European Commission Intelligent Information Interfaces (i3) programme. John and Iram Siraj-Blatchford have conducted a number of research projects together.

Margaret Still was an experienced primary teacher for many years, an advisory teacher for IT for eight years and was a part-time senior lecturer at Roehampton Institute for Education. She also acts as an independent education consultant and is a team inspector for Ofsted. She worked at BECTA for one year as a project officer and is a member of the publications group for MAPE. She has worked for over 40 years in the field of Primary Education, specializing in ICT.

Chris Taylor taught in primary schools for 15 years with a specialism in music. Subsequently he was an advisory teacher with Kent County Council. He then moved to teaching in higher education at Canterbury Christ Church and Exeter University. He is now retired but still works part-time for Devon Social Services, as an Ofsted Inspector and as a visiting lecturer at the Univesity of the West of England.

Mary Lou Thornbury is an experienced teacher of all age phases. She has been an advisory teacher and has worked as a higher education lecturer at the University of North London.

Tim Waller is Director of Postgraduate Studies in the Department of Childhood Studies at Swansea University. He was formerly at the School of Education, University College Northampton. Before that he taught in nursery, infant and primary schools in London and has also worked in the USA. He has been investigating the use of computers by young children for over eight years and completed his doctoral thesis on scaffolding young children's learning and ICT. Tim has a number of recent publications concerning the application of ICT in the teaching and learning of literacy.

David Wheway is currently a music adviser in Leicestershire and Northamptonshire. He is a partner of Leicestershire Music Publications providing Inset and publishing materials for early years and primary, to support the generalist teacher, classroom and early years' practitioners and parents. Since 1992 David has promoted Internet freeware to support PoS 5d, and been an ICT consultant to various national bodies and education authorities. He is a contributor to *Zone Magazine* and published a chapter in the 'ICT in Primary Schools' National Association of Music Educators (2004) publication, *How Can it Be Done?* entitled, 'Ideas In Music Out'.

David Whitebread trained as an early years teacher and worked in primary schools for 12 years before moving into higher education. He is presently a senior lecturer in the Faculty of Education, University of Cambridge, where he teaches and carries out research in early years education and psychology related to child development and education. His latest books include, *Teaching and Learning in the Early Years* (2nd edn) (RoutledgeFalmer 2003) and *Supporting Information & Communication Technology in the Early Years* (with John Siraj-Blatchford, Open University Press 2003).

John Woollard is a lecturer at the University of Southampton where his work focuses on ICT training for primary and secondary teacher trainees, and Masters teaching. He was a primary teacher before working in mainstream secondary special needs. His research focuses upon the use of icons and metaphors in the teaching of computing and computer learning by children and adults.

SERIES EDITORS' PREFACE

We might take as a principle of ICT in the classroom that it is only effective when integrated into existing good practice. It is fascinating to consider therefore how many early years practitioners have grappled with the problems of bringing together ICT and active learning and now provide us with models to explore our own practice.

We are delighted therefore that this volume provides an opportunity both to look at effective practices in the classroom and to consider the principles underlying effective ICT use in the field of early years teaching and learning. We are indebted to David Whitebread and Mary Hayes for their work as editors on this volume. Their vision of the ways in which early years education might be developed through the new potential of ICT is outlined below.

During the early phases of the introduction of ICT into education, there were many in the early years world who seriously doubted the appropriateness of computers and other information and communication technologies as a part of the educational provision for young children. The model of the passive child sitting mindlessly pressing buttons and being rather superficially entertained by fancy graphics on a screen seemed totally at odds with the ideal of the young child as an empowered, creative and active learner.

However, the situation is now very different. In many instances early years practitioners have moved from being the most sceptical to the most enthusiastic advocates of the educational value of ICT. By its very nature, being involved in the education of our youngest children is a creative and spontaneous enterprise. Practitioners in this age phase are, perhaps more than in any other, confronted explicitly on a daily basis with the complexities and realities of learning. As a consequence, they think deeply about it and are quick to identify experiences which seem to be beneficial to the young children with whom they are working. The model of the passive child in front of the computer screen only holds until one has actually experienced young children interacting with any form of technology, whether it is a programmable robot, a digital camera or a computer. Immediately, one witnesses the engagement, the social interactivity and collaboration, the creativity that is stimulated and the potential of ICT for young children's learning becomes very clear. Far from enslaving the young child, it is increasingly recognised that ICT has much to offer the child which is liberating, supports their conceptual development and puts them firmly in control of their own learning.

This book is inspired by the attempt to represent how this situation is currently being enacted in many early years settings and how it might be further developed. The chapters review work in a range of curriculum areas, but each starts from the research base relating to young children's learning and attempts to articulate important principles. While practical examples are described and discussed, the intention is not to promote particular applications, but rather to show how important principles can be played out in reality.

Our aim is to help early years practitioners, those currently training to work with young children, and those pursuing higher degrees to see the potential of particular ICT applications, to select those of most benefit to young children and to use them in ways which most powerfully support learning. Working with an ICT application should, like any other experience in an early years setting, encourage playfulness, present the child with a cognitive challenge, give a sense of control, and encourage creativity and personal expression. Beyond this, however, as is demonstrated in the chapters of this book, effective use of ICT applications offers young children opportunities to engage in powerfully enriching ways with various modes of expression and communication (such as language, visual arts, music and film), with verbal, mathematical and scientific thinking and problem solving, and with education about information and communicative technologies themselves (which is, of course, a vital aspect of preparing young children today for their future lives as citizens).

It has been a tremendous pleasure and privilege to work with all the contributors to this book, each of whom are established experts in their part of this growing and dynamic field.

As series editors, and both having secondary teaching backgrounds, we feel we have learned a lot about teaching and learning more generally while working on this early years volume. We hope that all readers of this book will find the contents both stimulating and helpful in developing their work using ICT with young children.

Anthony Adams and Sue Brindley

INTRODUCTION: TEACHING FOR TOMORROW

Mary Hayes

The intention of this book is to look at the teaching of ICT in the early years with a view to helping the teacher to consider how the special nature of ICT can be used in teaching to develop children's learning. The concept of 'teaching for tomorrow' is intended to convey the dual purpose of the book – to assist with teaching tomorrow's lesson, but also that it focuses on tomorrow's citizens. The children we teach today are the adults who will be determining our own futures 'tomorrow', and it is our responsibility to enable them to make informed choices and to be in control of the technology they will use. All teachers are aware that the ideas they discuss with a class of children today may be modified in the future by new approaches or discoveries. We cannot second-guess the future for the children we teach, but we can try to take an imaginative approach in our teaching and keep ourselves informed about how the present situation is changing. This chapter is concerned with one such aspect, that of globalization, which is considered in relation to the book as a whole.

Children today have the world in their living rooms through the medium of television. In the last century, technology enabled them to watch men landing on the moon and a robot moving around Mars. Banks of huge computers were seen at the space centre, with the anxiety and delights of the people working at them. Mistakes were clear to all too, when a space shuttle exploded not long after take-off, and were corrected in a subsequent space flight when a module was repaired in a space walk. The effect of these events has been to 'compress space and time' (Waters 1995). Children see events happening on the other side of the world at the same time that these events happen, and the images might seem to be given the same status as recorded events in our own locality. Children are able to use the Internet and email to build friendships and learn about other peoples' lives, thoughts, likes and aspirations. This aspect of talking to others using email is discussed in Chapter 3 by Waller, using daily communication across the globe. The chapter also focuses on how children in the future are likely to need to access a range of texts and will be aware that they can publish to the 'world'. Chapter 2, by Fine and Thornbury, concentrates on the social benefits of communicating with ICT as one aspect of the richness of the nursery environment. There are new social aspects to be explored when sharing experiences and collaborating with others who have differing cultural and linguistic experiences. Technology can aid the process of making the global village a reality.

Another aspect of space–time compression is experienced if children's carers can afford to take them to other countries. In just three hours they can be in a land that looks and smells different, with a complete change of temperature. Despite this, children often find familiar shops in the high street of the other country, and the food they eat abroad is often found in the supermarket at home. As well as shop similarities, there are product colours and logos that are recognizable, regardless of language differences; and the children's favourite toy craze might be advertised on television. People move around the world faster and it feels smaller as a result. However, children should be much more than the consumers of information. They need to develop the skills to critically analyse and respond to a wide range of evidence about the world around them, and learn about values and the experience of being human. The children of the future will be responsible for sustaining the European concept of Human Rights, which generally has global support.

When they become adults, today's children will be working with an element of risk, because as people use computers more, the situation goes beyond the five senses, and forces them to trust people they have never seen, such as the United Nations Organisation or the World Health Organisation. Through using the Internet they will read alternative views of the world and texts written in other cultural contexts, that are far away. They will need to be able to distinguish between texts that have a secure provenance and those that are based in fantasy.

In Chapter 5, by Feasey and Still, there is a discussion of how children can use ICT to develop their thinking and problem solving. They can 'experiment with world roles in models of real life problems' using a range of contexts. These activities help children to recognise which information is important, given a wide range of choices. It helps them to plan and work under time pressure and, most importantly, make mistakes in a safe environment. These three aspects reflect the results of handling and using information in society – information overload has been a consequence of the growth of the Internet combined with the speed of moving information from place to place; society has become highly organised due to the fact that it depends on information (Webster 1995); and knowledge itself has been treated as just a commodity, an aspect considered by Lyotard (1993), which I believe is an aspect that has led to errors in judgement. Experience gained in safe problem-solving situations will help to produce future citizens who will be aware of the importance of Webster's (1995: 105) words about information management in the 'public sphere', 'reliable and adequate information will facilitate sound discussion, while poor information . . . almost inevitably results in prejudicial decisions and inept debate'.

The use of ICT to access experiences that would otherwise be dangerous, time consuming or impossible, is considered in Whitebread's Chapter 6. This chapter strongly advocates the practical concrete experiences that are needed to build on, but also discusses using ICT to gain and record feedback from sensors. This concrete, real life experience is essential when the individual experiences a virtual event, such as those events in recent films (for example where a bus jumps an impossibly wide gap) in order that the children realise that the event is not actually a possibility in real life.

Giddens (1990: 64) suggested that globalization is 'the intensification of social relations which link distant realities in such a way that local events are shaped by events happening many miles away'. Children have witnessed disasters on television. They are aware of the ways in which adults use technology and respond to it. They have seen other children starving in Ethiopia and while they responded to *Blue Peter* appeals for action, the adults in their lives responded to pop groups who inspired people to work together to make a difference. This gives them a real opportunity to help to make a difference to the widening gap between the industrialised economies and the world's poor, a point discussed by Plant (2000). It is particularly important for children to find a way to respond to anxieties that may be created by such events. Research by Hicks and Holden (1995) uncovered the fact that although children had high aspirations for the future, they felt that there was little likelihood that they would be able to make a difference to global concerns such as polluting the environment. Personal empowerment is the theme of the first chapter, which advocates listening to what children have to say in order to help them to recognise their own ability to learn through and utilise ICT.

Children develop identity through their acquisition of social and cultural tools. Chapter 9 by Hayes, Taylor and Wheway discusses music as being socially and culturally essential, and is presented in terms of children developing confidence in a fun way through the development of listening and creating skills, memory and judgement. Chapter 1 discusses how teachers can support children in developing skills through the use of ICT and how the software itself is laden with messages. These messages or signs, are all around us, because of the spread of technology in our lives, as Webster (1995) suggests. The photographs on the walls of people's homes, he claims, are the biographies of people. Style and fashion are a projection of the individual, and we are bombarded with advertising images, style magazines and programmes. Everything we see has been altered, edited and constructed by people. In a discussion of the writings of Baudrillard, Webster (1995) argues that this is a social constructivist view of signs, that people are in fact creative in the way they watch television or use their computers and it is important now to experience these signs by manipulating and experiencing them for ourselves, rather than trying to interpret them. Another aspect of the use of signs is addressed in Chapter 7, by Cooke and Woollard. It reports on the issue of how children interpret symbols and icons in hardware and software. This adds to our knowledge about computer literacy, a theme developed by Marsh in Chapter 8. Visual literacy is an important aspect of learning for children since technology in the form of networked computers is now an integral part of both social and occupational life. Webster (1995) draws the analogy of a National Grid of computers to the motorways of recent times and the canals and railways of the previous era.

The emphasis in all the chapters of this book is on how the learner can be assisted to gain learning opportunities from changes in technology. Regular change is another aspect of globalization along with the realisation that knowledge must be considered to be always changing and therefore provisional. Chapter 4, by Bennett, discusses changes in technology in terms of constructivism, with an emphasis on the learner making sense of the activities to which they have access. He quotes Papert (1980) who was an early proponent of children being in control of the technology: 'the most useful sort of knowledge is that which enables the child to get more knowledge'.

Blatchford and Blatchford sum up our wishes for the early years ICT curriculum of the next century in Chapter 10. They explore the four aspects that children will need in a global future: communication and collaboration; creativity; metacognition; and learning to learn. If teachers can provide this most useful sort of knowledge, children will be better equipped to cope with the instability of a changing situation. Hopefully, this book will help readers to plan their teaching for tomorrow, but also and perhaps more importantly to think and plan differently longer-term for the citizens of tomorrow.

References

Giddens, A. (1990) *The Consequences of Modernity*. Cambridge: Polity.
Hicks, M. and Holden, C. (1995) *Visions of the Future*. Stoke on Trent: Trentham.
Lyotard, J-F. (1993) *Political Writings*. London: UCL Press.
Papert, S. (1980) *Mindstorms: Children, Computers and Powerful Ideas*. Hemel Hempstead: Harvester Wheatsheaf.
Plant, M. (2000) Unpublished PhD dissertation, Nottingham Trent University.
Waters, M. (1995) *Globalisation*. London: Routledge.
Webster, F. (1995) *Theories of the Information Society*. London: Routledge.

WHAT DO THE CHILDREN HAVE TO SAY?

Mary Hayes

Introduction

This chapter looks at the learning that takes place when young children use information and communications technology (ICT), seen here as computers and electronic toys. The toys can be cuddly, wearable, robots, toys that communicate or interactive books. The teacher's considerations need to be twofold, since Information Technology (IT) structures need to be addressed alongside the knowledge and understandings that are the main focus of learning through ICT. This chapter is contextualised by recent work in the field of developmental psychology, but that work is not reported here. The focus of this chapter is the children's knowledge about and experience of the use of computers *as expressed by the children themselves*. The work reports on how young children verbally construct their learning. The data does not represent adult constructions of children's learning, but allows the children to construct their own reports, so the language they use to construct their accounts may not be interpreted in the same way by adults as by children. Adults can, however, try to listen. The chapter also considers the things that children say about their use of electronic toys and computers. The question of pupil agency forms the central concern of the chapter.

What knowledge are we considering when children use computers?

One of the origins of the word educate claims to be from the Latin word 'educare' meaning 'to lead out'. I believe that this is the central purpose of early years' education – to draw out what the child knows and to lead them forward, in order for them to learn new things. I have chosen my words carefully here; the child is presented as the person who is active in the learning process. I have not used the word 'teach' because this chapter is not concerned with knowledge that the teacher can impart to the child, but with what knowledge the child is able to give to the teacher. The child is the learner and it is the learner that holds the key to what they know. The key is a metaphor used by Johnston (1996) in her studies of learning styles, and is a helpful one in this context. Just as you would give permission to a locksmith to assist you to enter your home when you are locked out, the child gives permission to the teacher to assist them in gaining entry to the learning process. Only when permission is given can the teacher's role in the education process really begin. Finding out what the child knows is a fundamental part of teaching and this is what assessment is about. Drummond (1993) writes comprehensively about the need to get inside the mind of the child in her discussion of the work of Jason, where instead of focusing on how little he achieves, she asks the reader to consider how much Jason knows through a thorough examination of his work. The elements of the assessment process in relation to computers are eloquently expressed elsewhere (Underwood and Underwood 1990; Loveless 1995) where the issues of careful observation, questioning, considering learning outcomes and attending to children's work are fully addressed. I am advocating here that instead of imposing our own views of what children should know, and looking for evidence of that, we listen to what children have to say and try to understand *their* ways of thinking and *their* perspectives. We need to hear what they have to say about how they construct their own view of the world.

Constructivism is a social view of learning developed from the work of Vygotsky (1978) and discussed in the context of education by Dewey (1966), Piaget (1973) and Bruner (1973), which implies (among other things) that when young children learn they go through a process of awareness, exploration, manipulation and interrogation, aided and encouraged by other humans. In other words they develop knowledge about something. This is referred to by James (1950) as 'knowledge about'; by Ryle (1949) as 'knowledge that'; and extended by Blackler (1995) as 'embrained', from Collins (1993). In the case of children learning through the use of ICT, the 'something' that they learn is mediated by a computer, so the knowledge becomes:

- knowledge of the computer itself;
- knowledge of something that can be learned through using the computer;
- knowledge of how we learn when using computers; or
- knowledge of how the use of computers affects people's lives.

In order to develop any or all of these kinds of knowing, depending on the learning context, differing understandings are needed. First, the understanding of what is regarded as IT – the channel through which learning occurs and, second, what is understood as ICT – the content of the learning with and without a communications network, are required for effective learning to take place (see Table 1.1).

My conception here does not quite fit the other notions of knowledge suggested by Blackler (1995), since a computer has aspects of 'embodied' knowledge due to being action-oriented, which allows children to do things; it is 'encultured', as it is a product of culture and used by culture as a symbol for other aspects of culture; it is 'embedded', due to the relationships between power, roles and emerging routines in our society; and it is 'encoded', since it uses signs and symbols for representations. When children learn something by using a computer they learn knowledge that is represented textually, mathematically, graphically, photographically or as simulation. Having understood that the representation is meaningful they then have to be able to access the material in the machine by utilising

Table 1.1 Different types of knowledge and levels of learning in ICT

Knowledge of computers (IT)	skills	conceptual structures (software)	conceptual structures (hardware)	program-writing	technical aspects
Knowledge through using computers (ICT)	skills	conceptual structures (software)	conceptual structures (hardware) sometimes	LOGO Control	sometimes
Knowledge of how computers affect lives	skills	conceptual structures (software)	sometimes - disability		
Knowledge of the learning process with computers	skills	conceptual structures (software)			

both physical and intellectual skills, techniques, concepts and attitudes. The act of using the computer may also stimulate emotional responses. It is a complex process where a number of different skills interact.

The following example of a child using a game provides a simple outline of the interaction of physical and intellectual skills. A young child would need to know how to switch on the machine and do some other task to load the software. They would then need to be able to use an input device to control the program and they would need to have some idea of the sequence of active possibilities in order to begin to manipulate or interrogate the ideas. They would also need the confidence to do it. The ICT ('learning through') therefore depends heavily on IT ('learning about'). While these kinds of actions may quickly become so well known that they are automatic, other complexities and subtleties then challenge the learner. For example, children need to learn about the structure of a database in order to be able to interrogate it effectively. But do children think about knowledge in the same way, and what do they think they know about computers and their use of computers?

Conversations with children

I decided to ask the children themselves what they knew about computers. I talked to a total of 67 children in three schools aged between 4 and 6 years old. I hesitate to use the term interview since it was sufficiently open to respond to the interest of each individual child, and was very informally carried out in the classroom context, rather as any other activity would be with a visiting helper. It was very much in the style described by Mayall (2000), best described as a conversation with the child. The children were fully informed by me of my interest – that I was interested to find out what they thought about learning with computers, that it was a study project rather like they might do in school, and that I was a learner like them. I told them that they did not have to answer my questions if they chose not to. Network analysis (Bernstein 1996) was used to analyse the children's conversations and four categories were developed that related to the knowledge categories described above. Some utterances may be considered in a number of ways – there is a multi-layered analytical frame. The next four sections in the chapter outline the children's comments in relation to the four categories.

Knowledge of the computer

In this very mixed socio-economic and culturally diverse group of children, about half said that they had computers at home. Interestingly the children described a wide range of machines as computers, including a range of games machines and 'toy' computers or television access. This was an important learning aspect for me, as of course in an early years setting there are many objects containing computer chips with which the children play. They do not hold the same distinctions of what 'computer' means as I do. The 4- and 5-year-olds referred to a very wide range of things that they called 'computers'. Like the 5-year-olds, the 6- and 7-year-old children referred to a wide range of machines as computers, but they also added comments about peripherals. 'All are virtually different – this one came with that [points to a scanner] – heaven knows what that is – Ruth's came with speakers; they all have different things on them' (Alex). They were either more aware of differences, or more able to describe them: 'The computer at home is different from this one . . . the new one [at home] has a really big screen and it's more powerful . . . the old one is in my bedroom but I can't get the Internet because there isn't a switch' (Ruth).

The 4- and 5-year-old children were able to talk about how they judged their learning in terms of general aspects of learning at home and school. The 6- and 7-year-olds were able to talk in terms of what they thought they learned from using computers specifically. Of the 6-year-olds, twenty one began the conversation with a personal focus, about their own use of the computer. Four talked in terms of affect – what their feelings were about it; four discussed it in an experiential manner – 'I have used the computer at school'; seven talked first in terms of ownership, and seven in active terms – what they could do with one. Three used an evaluative focus as the first response, judging its worth in their lives, and four distanced themselves from it, objectifying the computer in order to inform me about it.

In the 7-year-old group seventeen referred to the computer in these objectified terms, referring to what it is or how it can be used; only one used an evaluative focus as the first response and seven began with a personal focus only one referring to ownership, four talking about active aspects, one gave an affective response and a new term appeared – *know*. Within these objectified terms the computer was described in a number of ways:

- As a tool: 'you can print things' (Keiran).
- As an information source: 'you can find out things' (Fraser); 'you can learn things from them, like this program [he points to a CD-ROM] – you're learning things about the world and in the world' (Alex).
- As a source of fun: 'you can play games like the Magic School Bus' (Bethan); 'you need to have a disc to play games' (Tom).

The children explained that their knowledge is partly gained by observing others: 'I've seen my sister doing things for her projects' (Louise). Careful observations of other people using computers and experience is easily misinterpreted as idleness or an inability to concentrate, particularly if the child dashes over to the computer to have a look, then goes away. This observation will inevitably occur whenever a new version or peripheral appears: 'My dad's got a computer at home and he plays games and writing and he's got this thing and you can put photos in and put them into the computer' (Keith). Keith clearly had not yet learned what the scanner was called but he knew what it was for, while Bethan was struggling with correct terminology generally: 'My daddy uses a "psychypaedia". I watch him'. Only a quarter of the children used the correct terminology when talking about computers. These children were also those who had personal control of their computer use at home. This might indicate that their parents are adults who want them to know about things, so make an effort to help them to gain access to computers. The words used were: keyboard, mouse, keys, keypad, space bar, discs, Internet, load, email, CD, font, connected, screen saver, floppy, hard disc, D drive, joystick and password; all words associated with access to the computer. Ten children gave clear explanations of aspects of how to operate computers; this included how to switch on, the use of passwords, starting up the Internet, how to run a demonstration program, printing out, loading discs in different drives, loading and using email, loading a word processor, drafting and changing writing styles, loading and running CD-ROMs.

Home rules for the use of computers varied. In terms of whether or not they could use the computer, some were allowed to use it at any time, either alone, or with an adult or with a sibling. Others were allowed to use it only after the adults had done their work and their older children had completed homework. Two were not allowed to use it at all; Tom said, 'It's big; it's never used by the kids' and others were allowed to use it but not to switch it on or access programs. These issues are similar to those outlined by Downes and Reddacliffe (1999) in Australia who talked to young children that regularly used a computer at home. They reported on children's perceptions of access, ownership, rules and the ways children used the computers at home. The results clearly indicated the extent to which computers were a daily part of the children's lives. Selwyn and Bullon (2000), who also discuss issues of access at home, point out that not all young children take the opportunity to engage frequently with the technology, although all children spoken to, expressed a preference to use it regardless of the activity. Much other research has been carried out regarding children's learning, but it provides little evidence of the child's own views.

Knowledge of things learned by using a computer

As children are socialised into school they become more aware that adults have an agenda for their learning – socially, linguistically, culturally, behaviourally. They learn quickly what they must not do in order to avoid punishment. An adult frame of reference is quite different from that of a child and an incomprehensible response to questions may be purposeful, not ignorant or mischievous. Children need to be encouraged to frame their own questions. Pupil questions are a clear indicator of a number of aspects of learning – what pupils already know, what is important to them, how they sort information, how they go about problem solving, their preferred mode of approach to learning, and sometimes possibly levels of motivation. An approach to the encouragement of children's own questions in the classroom implies a valuing of the learner's views, letting the individual speak in the learning process. Many children understood that information could be obtained from the Internet or from CD-ROMs. Bhavisha was quite clear about the type of help she needed in order to progress, but talked in terms of home use:

> 'I learn things on my computer – I have two sorts of Encartas to learn . . . I play a game as well. I play the sort of game where they used to play the music in olden times, click on music and then it makes the sound. I've even got the Human Body. Next I would like to learn about the body because I look at it on my own [the CD-ROM] but I don't know what it is'

Children like Bavisha need to feel able to ask about things that they want to learn about, even if it is not one of the teacher's 'objectives' for the day.

Knowledge of how they learn when using computers

The children talked about both physical and conceptual aspects of learning. Physical skill was explained in terms of both ease and difficulty and described in relation to input devices: Fay talked about writing, 'It's a bit hard finding the letters because they're not in order [alphabetical]. I have a struggle finding some capital letters. I like doing pictures, I keep rubbing out because when you move the mouse you sometimes slip'. Paul explained a difficulty when using the mouse to draw pictures on the computer: 'when I move it sort of when I colour it in it goes out of the lines and it's a bit easier with the pencil. That's my rather squiggly ship'. Jade agreed – 'I did a picture on the computer at school – it goes all messy when you colour it in'. The mouse was also a source of trial for Sophie, 'It's quite hard because its stiff and when it gets moving it goes quite quickly' and for Peter, 'The mouse sort of goes a bit scribbly'. As well as pinpointing a spatial orientation relationship between the screen and the input device, Yasmin mentioned one of the promises that computers have long been expected to fulfil, the opportunity for uncritical repetition: 'The joystick goes the opposite way from the way you would want it to go on screen, it's a bit confusing. Father Christmas spins when the cards come rushing in which means you've lost your life. It doesn't matter because I can go on and play as the next person because nobody plays with me'. Other children, however, found certain uses of the computer easier: 'I like writing on computers. I like to write a story or poem, it's quite hard but I like it. When I show it to people they say it's quite good. The computer helps you because when you are typing something on the keyboard it's quite easy – it's hard to do letter shapes with a pencil' (Christiane). Adam commented on his use of the computer for pictures, game playing and writing, 'It is harder to try and do a picture – you can't put the line where you want to. It is easier playing games – playing games is easier than writing or drawing but it's harder than playing games'. The latter comment referred to table games or those available on the carpet in the classroom indicating that he was finding games played on the computer more conceptually challenging than those available in the classroom.

One of the aspects that made the use of computers difficult for children was their lack of understanding about the structure of the software. Sana was able to express her feelings about the difficulties involved when you just can't get entry to something that is new and outside your previous experience:

> When I was working on that computer [she points to the school one] I didn't know how to work on it because I didn't know how to work on it. On mine I put these games in. There are colourful pictures already there. I think and think 'what shall I do?' in my mind and I get scared. I want someone to help me.

Sometimes the children constructed assumptions about types of software. Rebecca said, 'I find playing one game hard'. On enquiring further I discovered that it was a game of chance. These particular children had not learned that in computer games there is often an element of chance. Sasha wanted to keep practising because her grandma always won. These children did not know that random events might have been programmed into a game, so they believed that if they just tried harder at the game that they would be sure to succeed. Cara showed that she did not register any difference between using a word-processing program and a game: 'I write, play games and it has a fish on it – when I fish it I can't find no fish in the sea. It's a game. Writing is easy. Fishing is hard'. Where these assumptions about the software structures go unchallenged, it can affect a child's self-esteem in relation to learning with computers. Despite being able to access information on the Internet, Paul felt that he wasn't really very good with computers. A sticking point for him was games: 'I normally need help when I do some games, often I don't get it right. In windows – I put these cards in the right order and it's really hard to get them right'. In order to raise the level of confidence in their own abilities, children need to be informed about differences between the different types of software structures.

There were other intimations about levels of confidence when using computers. Eighteen children mentioned the word 'hard' in relation to using computers. Despite this, they showed an interest in being able to use them more often. Three used the word 'like' in relation to using computers, four said that they were good at using them and seven proclaimed them to be fun. Ruth expressed a high level of confidence: 'I'm good at drawing on the computer. I know how to get at most things on that program. I'm good at writing pad but extremely good at the paint program. My dad taught me when I was 5 or 6. I'm good at drawing. When I was 5 I used to draw all the time'. When I asked her what made her so sure that she was good she replied: 'Because all the years past I've been drawing and had very close memories from that point. Mum tells me I was good at it and says I was good then. She tells me most things I used to do as a kid'. I asked how else she knew. 'I know myself – like drawing – I practise lots, I've drawn millions at home'. Ruth was not the only child that claimed self-knowledge – Fraser said, 'I've been able to do it [drawing on the computer] since I was 4 years old and because I've done it with my dad he showed me when I was 3 – I couldn't do it for a year but when I was 4 I could'. Rachel remembered learning about computers, 'I learnt and tried when I was very small. My mum told me how to do it and she encouraged me'. Jamie was particularly pleased with his work at school, 'I've done a picture on it – it was quite easy – it was probably the best picture I've done'. All the children except two referred to learning taking place at home. There were three origins of learning mentioned by the children:

1 A memory of always being able to do it
2 Observing others or through experimentation
3 Being shown or taught by other people.

The children mentioned a number of people that helped them to learn to use computers. One child mentioned learning from a teacher and another learning from a nursery teacher who was in charge of after-school childcare. The others located their learning firmly in the home: parents and siblings, grandparents and friends were all mentioned. This is not surprising, given the greater opportunities to interact with people on a one-to-one basis at home.

Knowledge of how computers affect peoples' lives

The children had knowledge of how computers affect peoples' lives. Jamie explained the effect on the whole family, 'I play games on it like for school and that like helps you. It helps my brother do his work. My mum is opening a hair salon and it's helping her too. We play games; my brother goes to a computer fair. My grandad's got a typewriter and it does the same'. Tanya showed a touching faith in the power of computers when she engaged in some wishful thinking in relation to computer use, 'I'd be interested in winning the lottery'.

The children also made social references – 'you can go on the Internet and explore stuff – if you hear on TV www.cbbc.co.uk you just go on it and find out about a program' (Christopher); or 'I watched this program about some children and I think they were working on the Internet'. There was also evaluative social commentary – 'computers are clever because look at that [clicks on the screen to start an animation sequence] the people who make it are clever – they make so many games' (Alex).

How far are young children able to take control?

A study by Dann (1996) in discussing the need for dialogue to ensure mutual understanding suggests that it is crucial that children get opportunities to express the rationale behind their thinking. That is what these children were doing. The children had very clear awareness of their own difficulties and achievements. This awareness expressed itself in different ways. First, they compared themselves with other people, friends and siblings; or compared one task to another; five children identified criteria that they used for judging their own work when talking about pictures. They mentioned detail, colour, balance and decoration; one child talked about comparing her drawing with the original object, holding the flower next to the screen, and one said that he knew that his picture was not good when things went wrong. Second, some children analysed difficulties in terms of physical skills with a mouse, and reading difficulties. Third, several children gave evidence of what they saw as progress by referring to the stages provided within computer games or mathematical or reading 'next step' (learning the next spelling card), while one mentioned 'doing it all by me own' as an example of progress; surprisingly only one child mentioned the smiley face as a form of feedback, so perhaps it is the response of the person giving it that matters more than the smiley face. Fourth, five children reported on what they had experienced in order to learn. They mentioned listening, remembering, practising, watching and thinking, or 'using your brain', and one mentioned gaining rewards. The evidence from my conversations with young children has shown that they are capable of knowing about different types of learning involved when using computers and that they are capable of clarifying to adults their learning about using computers, albeit that they are at a wide range of different capabilities.

Concluding issues

Since children are able to express these aspects of their own learning process, we should be asking them much more often about what they have done before and what kinds of things they would like to learn about. Children need to be tackling very different tasks, if they begin with a more highly developed level of confidence and competence with electronic toys and computers. The 'teacher' is only one of the many people who help young children. We need to remind ourselves frequently that children first learn about learning at home, and that we should be asking ourselves how we can know what those early experiences are and how we can help the children to build on them. This is a point made strongly by Wellington (2001).

The children in my sample were learning more about computers from home, their peers and the community, than from school. Outside school is where children are allowed more personal choice too. Could it possibly be that the actions the children take outside school are actions that build on their own tacit knowledge of what they already know? This is what children have done for years in play situations, but the school context has as yet not used much play related to computers in everyday life. Hayes and Johnson (1990) reported a study of a catalogue shop activity in a nursery. The activity used a play area with a computer as central to the context. The context was one that imitated normal life, and the learning that came out of the play activity surprised the teachers. The point is, that children were playing and making choices about the activities that would develop their personal experience and their tacit knowledge. A sensitive teacher will use this tacit knowledge, combine it with children's questions, and their own knowledge of the learning possibilities with computers and electronic toys. The teacher can use their knowledge to intervene with the child's permission, and help the child to learn more.

These conversations with children have restated the importance of considering aspects of learning that have long been a central concern for the early years' teacher. These aspects relate to the 'whole child' – linguistic elements, physical skills, social and affective aspects of learning, but this time with electronic toys and computers. New objects of use to learning provide new elements for consideration in the learning process – those of the conceptual structures in the software. The software is a product of the culture, while creating culture, but has a history that is related to the technical development of computers. This is perhaps why access to software can sometimes be inconsistent, eccentric and far from intuitive. If access is not to hinder children who have limited time to explore computers and electronic toys, teachers need to consider the software structure when working with children. Table 1.2 shows the conceptual elements to take into account when considering the use of a particular item of software. There are three groups of considerations:

WHAT DO CHILDREN HAVE TO SAY?

1. Aspects of IT – physical needs, vocabulary terms
2. Human needs – social considerations, emotional responses
3. Conceptual demands – both of the task challenge and of the software structures that relate back to children's misunderstandings.

Both IT and ICT are necessary for effective learning to take place. The learning needs to consider what the children know; how they feel about that; how they relate to other children; how interested they are in the whole process; how well they feel; and many other things. Once the

Table 1.2 Planning for ICT and the types of learning involved

Area of learning:

	Watching	Exploring	games	Single skills in context	Using template in context	More complex tasks	Child selection and choice
Physical skill							
Language							
Social aspects							
Emotional aspects							

		Watching	Exploring	games	Single skills in context	Using template in context	More complex tasks	Child selection and choice
Software Structure (IT)	Access							
	organisation							
	Random or not?							
	Ordered or free?							
	Comms?							
Content (ICT)								

teacher knows about the children as learners, they can be supported within a learning environment that takes all those bits of information into account. As the children use that environment to learn, the teacher observes and interacts with the children to help the child to gain confidence to develop and learn more.

The conversations with children have also raised the question of what type of opportunities teachers can provide to help children to become more confident and effective users of computers. The sort of opportunities suggested by the children's comments are:

- to have the chance to observe sufficient examples of computers in use by other people who have a greater knowledge of how to use them;
- to play with and explore programs and electronic toys, so that they are able to build up an understanding of what they know about and can do with computers and electronic toys;
- to acknowledge other 'teachers' in the child's life;
- to help children find out about new electronic developments;
- to teach them how to make choices and decisions;
- to encourage them to share their knowledge and opinions about their work with computers.

Research by Deloache and Brown (1987) indicated that children were more competent at handling their work – devising and using strategies – when the problems had been set by the pupils themselves or the work focused on familiar everyday life activities. Boud (1988) claimed that a learner will be effective when able to 'make decisions about what they should be learning and how they should be learning it'. Zimmerman and Kitzantas (1997) suggested that there may be evidence for developmental phases in self-regulation, with a shift from process goals to outcome goals. They claimed that complex cognitive–motor skills are difficult to learn on one's own – evidence of effectiveness is hard to interpret, or the evidence becomes clear to the learner so long afterwards that it is difficult to learn from. This implies that the teacher and child need to work side by side to find the key to that particular child's learning. Tunstall and Gipps (1996) characterised one type of teacher feedback as 'constructing achievement' due to the 'mutual articulation of achievement . . . the additional use of emerging criteria . . . and praise as integral to description'. They reported that teachers who used this type of feedback tended to use approaches that seemed to pass control to the child.

Plato, Dewey and Marx argued for a reproductive role of education. They were not at the time, aware of computers. Computers are opening the door to new knowledge. I am not claiming that old knowledge is irrelevant or unimportant, but only that children should be encouraged to think for themselves, that computers introduce new fast learning which requires more than a reproductive role since that would not equip children sufficiently for the future. It would only give them patterns to follow which could soon be obsolete. We should attempt to work with children to generate statements about their thinking, which can be viewed as propositions. We can compare their ideas with what happens and with other pupil's ideas to help them to reflect. This becomes even more urgent as young children begin to access the World Wide Web, since they will find enormous stores of information from which to select. They need secure teacher guidance on what sites are appropriate; what questions they want to ask; what specifically they want to know; and how to decide from the myriad options available. Most importantly, they will need help to know what they want to do with that information. The outcome of pupils reflecting and explaining their own knowledge-building processes could be that of personal empowerment. If we are to develop thinking citizens for tomorrow, then they need to play an active part in shaping their own futures.

References

Bernstein, B.B. (1996) *Pedagogy, Symbolic Control and Identity: Theory, Research Critique*. London: Taylor and Francis.

Blackler, F. (1995) Knowledge, work and organisations: An overview and interpretation, in D.J. Hickson and S.R. Clegg (eds) *Organisation Studies* (Issue 6). New York: Walter de Gruyter.

Boud, D. (ed.) (1988) *Developing Student Autonomy in Learning*. London: Kogan Page.

Bruner, J.S. (1990) *Beyond the Information Given*. London: George Allen and Unwin.

Collins, H. (1993) The structure of knowledge, *Social Research*, 60: 95–116.

Dann, R. (1996) Teacher–mentor to teacher–researcher, *Mentoring and Tutoring*, 3(3): 33–7.

Deloache, J.S. and Brown, A. (1987) The early emergence of planning skills in children, in J. Bruner and H. Haste (eds) *Making Sense: The Child's Construction of the World*. New York: Methuen.

Dewey, J. (1966) *Democracy and Education*. New York: Free Press.

Downes, T. and Reddacliff, C. (1999) *Young Children Talking about Computers in their Homes*. Available at http://www.spirit.com.au/ACEC96/papers/downe.htm (accessed 15 July 2000).

Drummond, M.J. (1993) *Assessing Children's Learning*. London: David Fulton.

Hayes, M. and Johnson, E. (1990) IT in the nursery – a new perspective, *Information Technology and Learning*, 13(2).

James, W. (1950) *The Principles of Psychology*. New York: Dover.

Johnston, C.A. (1996) *Unlocking the Will to Learn*. California: Corwin Press.

Loveless, A. (1995) *The Role of I.T.* London: Cassell.

Mayall, B. (2000) Conversations with children, in P. Christensen and A. James (eds) *Research with Children: Perspectives and Practices*. London: Falmer Press.

Piaget, J. (1973) *The Child's Conception of the World*. London: Kegan Paul.

Ryle, G. (1949) *The Concept of Mind*. London: Hutchinson.

Selwyn, N. and Bullon, K. (2000) Primary school children's use of ICT, *British Journal of Educational Technology*, 31(4): 321–32.

Tunstall, P. and Gipps, C. (1996) How does your teacher help you to make your work better? Children's understanding of formative assessment, *The Curriculum Journal*, 7(2): 185–203.

Underwood, J. and Underwood, G. (1990) *Computers and Learning*. Oxford: Basil Blackwell.

Vygotsky, L.S. (1978) *Mind in Society: The Development of Higher Psychological Processes*. Cambridge, MA: Harvard University Press. (Published originally in Russian in 1930).

Wellington, J. (2001) Exploring the secret garden: The growing importance of ICT in the home, *British Journal of Educational Technology*, 32(2): 233–44.

Zimmerman, B.J. and Kitzantas A. (1997) Developmental phases in self regulation: Shifting from process goals to outcome goals, *Journal of Educational Psychology*, 89(1): 29–36.

2
ICT: PLAY AND EXPLORATION

Carol Fine and Mary Lou Thornbury

> First of all there was the discovery that one of the greatest 'reinforcers' is the response of another human being ... The second thing [after that] infants seem to need was self initiated activity.
>
> (Bruner 1996: 9–10)

Bruner identifies two key factors in infant learning (Bruner, 1996: 9–10) the children's need, first, for adult responsiveness and, second, for self initiated activity. The responses of adults confirm the child's search for 'predictive stability' on the basis of which children take initiatives that extend further their knowledge of the world. As communicators of their culture, parents and teachers of early years children provide both the responsive environment and the arena for children to explore.

In this chapter we consider how information communications technology (ICT) can be part of a learning environment ('interaction and self initiation') which promotes worthwhile and novel learning experiences in the early years. Furthermore, we will examine how ICT can help in providing a firm basis for the acquisition of 'the tools of the culture' including reading, writing and arithmetic. As to the nature of that culture Meek (1982) writes: 'From the stories we hear as children we inherit the feeling mode, the truth value, the codes, the rhetoric, the transmission techniques that tell us who we are'.

Intent on communicating the 'tools' or 'transmission techniques' we should not lose sight of the children themselves and how they best learn. Clare and David Mills, in a groundbreaking study and television programme in 1997 (Mills and Mills 1997), argued that the teaching of young children should aim at slowly consolidating knowledge and confidence with the concrete, before moving on to representational material. They contrast the early years experience of children in Britain with that of Hungarian and Flemish-Belgian children who enter primary school at 7 having received no teaching at all in reading and writing and yet within one term, 'almost every normal Hungarian and Flemish-Belgian child can read and write'. As Mills and Mills assert, 'to British eyes the progress made is staggering' (1997: 13).

Our emphasis in this paper will be on the holistic development of the child's disposition to learn. We will look at the role of different types of software and their possible use in relation to the learning dispositions of children. We will give examples or 'case studies' of the use of different programs and a critique of the extent to which they establish secure learning patterns with potential for creative exploration. We shall also examine the computer not just as a form of transmission but to see if implicit in the design and content of the software are messages about the culture being transmitted.

One of the advantages of working with children using computers is that we, as teachers and researchers, benefit from the fact that computers make transparent the engagement of children: 'Computers have made pupil interactions visible to researchers . . . ways of using new educational technology brought a social psychological phenomenon into focus' (Crook 1998).

Case study: Using a paint program with 5–6-year-olds

A group of 30 children were given the opportunity to work in a 20-station computer suite for a morning. The prior experience of the children was of working with one computer in the classroom – a popular activity, but a rare one for individuals because of the ratio of computers to children. Some of the children had access to a home computer but it is difficult to determine what they did on their home computers. As with any other activity such as painting or reading, the home experience is very different from the school experience.

The children were introduced to a paint program by the teacher. This educational paint program has many exciting features, particularly the use of sound, stamps and paintbrush novelty patterns and a slide-show facility. The teacher used a digital projector or whiteboard to project the computer screen.

This facility is important in offering young learners a model of how to work when they go to the computer stations.

The teacher introduced the program slowly and in carefully measured steps, she explained how she loaded it, how to use the major paint tools and how to find a new page. At each stage the instructions were repeated and the children were asked to repeat to the teacher how particular operations were carried out, such as use of the fill tool or getting a new page. It is interesting to note that all the children sat attentively, listening and watching. This would have been impossible without the digital projector. The careful introduction of the activity gave the children opportunities for demonstrating attention, listening and memory.

The teacher was acting as a role model and giving children the confidence to become practitioners themselves. She was offering an activity which was imaginative and enjoyable and giving the children skills to develop their autonomy and disposition to learn. The software selected also encouraged the children to think creatively and imaginatively and to experiment and investigate in a safe environment, promoting playful engagement.

After the introduction the children were given the choice of working on their own at a computer or with a partner. They were able to go to a computer, load the program and begin to experiment entirely independently. Some children chose a partner but nearly all the children discussed their work with the person next to them and experimented with different paint tools, demonstrating them to each other. This gave them the opportunity to work alone and in small groups.

Experience on the Headstart programme (Hopper and Lawler 1997) would indicate that children learn best in 'a relatively unstructured and relaxed independent learning environment' after:

- a brief period first of adult instruction; then
- a brief period of adult supervision; followed by
- independent use alone and then with peers.

At this stage in the session the layout of the room was important in giving the children space around each computer. The computers were on benches round the edge of the room allowing the teacher to see all of the children's work and to identify if anyone needed help. In fact, the introduction had prepared most of the children well enough for them to proceed on their own until they needed to print their pictures. There were children with special educational needs in the group who were also able to carry out the activity with very little support.

Discussion

This case study directs attention to hardware, software and classroom organization.

Reception children do not usually have access to computer suites. Teacher trainees taking up their first post have reported that many of the schools they are working in do not timetable the computer suites for nursery or early years children. That there could be difficulties for young children in using a suite set up with older children in mind is touched on in a recent study from Newcastle which looked at effective pedagogies using ICT (Moseley et al. 1999). Yet frequently the establishment of a computer suite has taken resources and left the youngest children with out-of-date or no computers.

The main advantage in the case study was that the children were able to sit as a class group and view the digitally projected computer screen in comfort. Nevertheless, this was not a straightforward delivery model of learning; the children were encouraged to read together menu items on screen and direct where the teacher should click the mouse to produce a particular outcome. This gave the learning a social context. It encouraged the children to listen and co-operate in a structured group situation. They were learning the need to control impulses and understand the need for rules in a whole class learning environment. From our experience with initial teacher trainees we judge that teachers are much more willing to use ICT in their subject teaching if they have access to a digital projector or whiteboard.[1]

The teacher was also planning 'challenging opportunities for children whose ability and understanding are in advance of their language and communication skills' (DfEE 1999: 13). It also provided different tools for experimentation providing for those who may not work easily in other classroom media. A great advantage of this arrangement was the provision for the children to practise their newly observed skills immediately following the demonstration, reinforcing their memory of the instructions. Even in a traditional nursery or reception classroom there would be only one or two computers and the follow up exploration would be delayed for most children.

Software

Paint programs allow children to extend the experimentation with line and colour, which they have been making from their earliest years using paint, plasticine, crayons and clay, as well as offering tools such as stamps and animation which have not been previously accessible to young children.

Teachers need programs for early years children, written with attractive and exciting tools. Very young children can experiment with the mouse to draw and paint without needing to work with any text. Using a paint program is an ideal way of introducing the basic features of the computer and accustoming children to the use of icons and buttons. The software includes the use of sound and colour and gives access to children who are not yet reading and writing. In this situation it provided 'opportunities to motivate, support and develop children and help them to be involved, concentrate and learn effectively' (DfEE 2000: 18).

The program develops creativity: the children begin with a blank page and produce a unique and original piece. Many early learning programs used in schools provide children with games and stories and are mainly reactive. Although such programs are classified as 'interactive' the children are given choices but don't contribute to the program or change it. This may spring from the misconception by program designers that a good early learning program allows children to work without initial tutoring (which really means they can work without the adult interaction we have proposed as a prerequisite for learning), thus interpreting independent learning as being teacher-free. This often deprives the children of the opportunity to use the power of the computer to create something of their own. It also deprives them of the opportunity to test adult responses; the computer may go some way to providing these responses but only within the terms of its own programming.

Artistic development

Introducing a paint program enables children to understand that the computer is not just a tool for accessing information but that it is also a tool for creativity. We are talking about children working in the areas of art, graphics, sound and animation. These are media with which they are already acquainted when they come to nursery or school. A paint program enables them to understand how such media can be created and changed. The children are active learners and are making decisions about colour, sound or pattern in order to communicate.

Postman (1993: 121) reminds us that creativity can be lost by using computers. He writes, 'We know that doctors who rely entirely on machinery have lost skill in making diagnoses based on observation'. Perhaps our greatest commitment to the next generation is to enable children to control the new technologies rather than to be controlled by them.

Increasingly it is pictures rather than text which carry meaning in both the adult and the children's world. It is also pictures that reinforce stereotypes and exclude certain sectors of society. Children will learn that in pictures there are likely to be the selections and omissions that there are in stories. Teachers are used to pointing out if a story represents the mother doing the housework and the father washing the car; now teachers and children's attention must be drawn to Mrs Rabbit baking the cakes on the CD-ROM, while Roger Rabbit has an adventure. It is by making pictures that children learn that pictures are made just as text is made. It is such early experiences which should help children to be critical consumers of visual bombardment just as an earlier generation became critical readers of print.

In the next case study we will be looking at an example of an interactive learning tool for the early years and examining the messages children will take in with the learning.

Case study using a CD-ROM: The computer for exploration and feedback

This case study is based on our observation of children using a CD-ROM especially designed for them. The chief character is a little boy pig who takes the user around the farmyard to invite animals to his party. It is this character who works with the children; there is not the impression of there being an adult monitor. There are a number of motivating activities in the CD-ROM which can be used independently by children as young as 3- or 4-years-old once they have the basic mouse skills. It is also motivating for developing those mouse motor skills, including some very simple click and drag skills (e.g. the matching game). The games are chosen by the children and there is no imposition or withholding of 'certificates' validating the child's achievement in adult terms.

Some features include simple, well drawn graphics, a variety of farmyard characters with different voices and accents, well composed music and a range of activities geared to different skills but all accessible for this age group. The children can stop a game at any time by clicking on the pig and can exit the CD at any time by clicking on the 'bye-bye bird'. Children are entertained by this CD-ROM as solitary players but when they play together they discuss their decisions and choices. However, young children prefer at first to play with an adult and they play with parents or teachers to confirm their initial understanding of the purposes and potential of the activity.

All the children we have seen use this particular CD-ROM say 'Hello' to the pig at the beginning and identify with his quest to invite friends to a birthday party. They very quickly learn how to go round the farm before clicking on the pig's hat to go to the party and hear the 'Happy Birthday' song.

So how does this CD-ROM offer a unique learning experience besides the lower level ICT skills? The children have to listen carefully to instructions given in a perhaps unfamiliar accent. They are encouraged to make choices about where to visit on the farm and develop their independence of choice. They are, in fact, in control of their exploration; they choose which feature to click on or which game to pursue or leave. One 3-year-old returned over and over again to the dancing spoons with their jazz tune while a 4-year-old loved to catch the cats by clicking so as to see them drink their milk.

The tasks are well designed in that the children must understand them to complete them, and they do not lend themselves solely to trial and error solutions: there is the possibility for children to plan. Also important for young learners is the fact that each animal has been given a clearly defined character

ICT: PLAY AND EXPLORATION

Figure 2.1 Active ICT

which offers an early introduction to the recognition of character in story and can also give models for role-play.

The children are also introduced to the vocabulary of the farmyard: the barn, field, farmhouse and pond all have their relevant spoken vocabulary. When the children use this CD-ROM they are entering into an imaginary world where the choices they make offer a variety of feedback; they are being introduced to computer modelling. The layout of the CD-ROM is an early map in itself and the children see representation and symbol and orientate themselves accordingly.

Discussion: Quality of software

Although this is an example of a successfully designed CD-ROM it is not without its drawbacks. The main protagonist is an animal but it is still being given the male gender identity universal in the world of technology. This is compounded by the stereotypical roles given to some of the female animals. The cat in the farmhouse is given a deliberately flirtatious and rather seductive tone while the duck schoolteacher at the pond is made to sound 'upper class' and 'bossy', validating the raspberries of the naughty boy ducklings. Unfortunately the only time the child is required to recognise letters is at the very old-fashioned duck school where the alphabet is on the blackboard (not on a computer!) The children are required to practise drawing their letters with a mouse and a very thin pencil only – an activity which challenges the average adult. The message in this game is that print is difficult and it is transmitted through unattractive role models.

The drawing and painting is difficult with the mouse and the clock task in the kitchen setting is obscure. But the CD-ROM offers a foundation for visual and auditory literacy. Apart from the duck school, there is no text and the children learn to recognise that pictorial symbols have meaning. Listening becomes important: the spoken words also have meaning. The articulation of the characters is clear and the drawings simple and attractive. The variety and interest of the games and the different styles of learning are unusual in a CD-ROM. The sound effects are amusing and there are exclamations which indicate right or wrong guesses without being negative. One game does introduce symbols – the numbers 1 to 4. The other matching games on the whole require the children to be able to distinguish visual differences, an important pre-reading skill, a precursor of letter shape and word recognition. It is easy to exit from these games, unlike the games in many other CDs aimed at the same age group. It is possible for activity CD-ROMs aimed at early years children to be open and explorative but in our experience it is rare and this is one of the few that children continue to explore and enjoy.

Exploration and language

The computer is a rich and motivating resource for promoting literacy. In the painting case study the children were listening intently to instructions from the teacher and to each other as they experimented. The computer also offers the revelation of story where the children control the pace and interact with text, graphics, animation and sound. At a more creative level, the computer offers children the means of making their own stories and text. Educational word processors feed back text through sound as well as offering word banks for scaffolding writing with early learners.

This quite simple technology is offering access to literacy for children with particular special needs in a way that has not been available to other generations.

The CD-ROM has also changed the way in which children can access stories, exploratory games and rhymes in the early years classroom. Very young children now have access to sound, graphics, animation and video to excite them and motivate their reading and language development. With the computer growing in importance as a resource for language and literacy the evaluation of software becomes a necessary pedagogical tool.

If a child finds a book in the book corner which has no point of reference or with which they are unable to empathise they will select an alternative. The purchase of a CD-ROM still represents a considerable investment as part of the class budget and there will be less choice for the child. Thus, the lure of the sound and animation of the CD-ROM may mask deficiencies in story line, character, sequence of events or description. It may also portray stereotyped characters and situations which may be unacceptable.

The nature of CD-ROM technology means that the available material on each CD-ROM can be massive, so the task of evaluating each CD-ROM in order to identify the learning potential before use requires a considerable amount of time. So many of these CD-ROMs can be used independently by very young children that the task of evaluation is of great importance to ensure that with so few CD-ROMs in each classroom the children have access to the best in terms of quality of writing and presentation. It is easy for the overall impression to be attractive with many surface features such as animation and sound when plot, structure, characterisation and use of language are undemanding. The teacher would also wish to avoid the accessing of unsuitable features such as racist or gender stereotyping.

'talking book' CD-ROMs

Recent research on children using 'talking books' does indicate that with a high quality program there are significant gains for children's reading of new words and understanding of sentence and story.

One study (Cox 2000: 15) looks at Frank Smith's distinction between 'Top–Down' and 'Bottom–Up' approaches to reading and defines the gains with using Talking Books as being in the 'Top–Down' category of the holistic approach to reading while reinforcing 'Bottom–Up' skills of 'look-and-say' word identification. Cox quotes Medwell:

> Talking Books had helped children make sense of the texts and provided words that fitted the sentences meaningfully and grammatically. They did not however pay greater attention to the way the words looked and sounded. This finding suggests that talking stories support children's reading by offering them access to the meaning of the stories and the way the sentences work – a priority for shared reading.
>
> (Cox 2000: 6)

Cox in her observations of children found a difference in reading learning when children used CD-ROMs with clear bold text uncluttered by pictures. When comparing children using different talking books she observed that children looked at the words and played with the animation of one particular talking book but with another they tried to read. The latter example had clear, large type which was highlighted when the words were being read; the words were not blended into the background drawings but stood out clearly.

Cox evaluates the impact of the CD-ROMs on children's reading:

> The illustrations, animations and sound effects in talking books give meaning to the story and encourage children to look at books, which makes them particularly important for reluctant readers ... but while the words are being read and highlighted no animation should be playing.

The impact on early years children of an initial orientation to reading will be to give all children, boys particularly and those with auditory and visual impairments, access to story and are a motivating factor in encouraging all children to identify themselves as readers.

Mathematical understanding

There are great numbers of mathematically focused games in early learning software. Counting, matching, sorting, sequencing and shape recognition are all skills tackled by commercial software producers. However, it is sometimes difficult to judge how these games bridge the gap between the vital concrete experiences and abstract thinking. Watching children play some of these games we have wondered whether the reinforcement they provide adds to their mathematical knowledge. Are these games simply testing the children and if so how does the computer provide new things for the children to learn?

For example, the task which requires the children to match the number 4 to four objects does not prove that they can count to 4 or understand the symbol. It is a drill and practice task which has historically been carried out with cardboard and pictures in nursery classrooms and to which the computer can add sound, animation and feedback. The computer adds to this reinforcement a mode of learning which is novel in the early years classroom. It scaffolds the children's independent work and offers feedback without the presence of an adult. But the learning may simply be in the successful completion of the task, not in the understanding of numbers. Children are taught to match letters of the alphabet to pictures by dragging the picture until they get the tinkly sound of success (and the reward in points), but when questioned afterwards the link between the initial letter and the word identifying the picture had not been understood at all. However, the program had not been the subject of a class introduction.

An answer to this might be to use open-ended tools already known to the children. If we take the painting program referred to earlier and give the children an activity which requires them to use the stamps to make groups of three, four, five and so on, and then find the relevant symbol to match their set, then the quality of the learning experience is richer. The names of the numbers are reinforced by being spoken. This activity would be more likely to ensure learning for all children against the potential for error of the drill and practice. The teacher who described this activity said:

> The program was quite different from anything I've used before because the programs we've used before to support literacy were very closed . . . We didn't have much in the way of numeracy materials, whereas using the painting program has really helped, and the children have used a lot more mathematical language.
>
> (Moseley et al. 1999: 3)

Control: Programmable robots, play and discovery

But another and probably the most innovative and exciting mathematical tool which technology has made available to young children is the controllable robot. This is a tool to develop mathematical language, the understanding of numbers, including large numbers and the awareness of measuring movement in space. '[The idea that mathematics is to do with the body] has inspired me to use the computer as a medium to allow children to put their bodies back into their mathematics' (Papert 1993: 31). A robot is very much a transitional object; it can be personalised and given an identity, and the children transfer to the robot their understanding of how they move in space and how they measure that movement. In this way their understanding of direction and measurement becomes more objectified, more abstract; it is a way of making the transition from action to representation.

Richard Bennett in Chapter 4 in this volume states that 'how children come to associate abstract symbols through first hand experience is through E–L–P–S (Experience–Language–Pictures–Symbols)'. The robot is a tool for the early years teacher who wishes to extend their pupils' *experience* in the area of geometry. It will also 'reveal how the children use *language* in identifying their goals and planning their solutions' (Fine and Thornbury 2000: 128, emphasis added).

The use of the programmable robot will introduce concepts of space, direction, number and measure in ways that were not previously available in early years classrooms.[2]

By giving instructions to a floor robot children will be making things happen. The children need to enter an instruction using the keypad on the robot in order to make something happen. In the case of the programmable robot the instructions or commands are composed of a direction and a number. The distinction between the command and the number, which is its measurement, is crucial for young learners as they are learning about space in terms of the direction, and measurement in terms of number. The distinction between the command and the amount enables children to work in a mathematical environment in a way that was not available in schools before the development of this technology.

It is fascinating to see even very young children conquer the sequence of key presses required in order to make the robot move. By performing a sequence of instructions to make something happen and to control the robot they are at the first stage of programming.

The great advantage of using programmable robots with young children is that they are play objects and meet Bruner's requirement that 'infants seem to need self initiated activity' (Bruner 1996: 10). After an initial introduction of the robot, children will very quickly take ownership and experiment and play with the robot. Such play involves a great deal of social learning, turn taking and discussion as well as spatial awareness, recognition of numerals, practice with measurement, sequencing commands and logical thinking. The language used will include position and direction as well as number and estimation.

To give instructions in order to make something happen requires a goal, a plan and a language. Papert (1980: 22, 23) has pointed out that until relatively recently our culture has not given children opportunities to think and talk about problems systematically. The role of the floor robot in promoting the children's experimentation is unique. Unlike any other toy or construction game in the nursery we observed children defining aloud a goal or purpose in order to 'play' with the robot. Successive groups of nursery children working in pairs identified the place they wanted the robot to reach and then commanded it to move. The robot was given a role, a personality and a story as they played.

One aspect of the robot play in the nursery was the relative speed with which the children learned the grammar of a robot command. By the third or fourth session children were able to program a sequence of instructions instead of separate movements and they became confident using larger numbers, such as thirties and forties. All this work involved intense discussions and the formulation of commands using precise language.

One 5-year-old boy in a reception class discovered that a command of left or right 90 would result in his robot 'turning a corner'. When challenged to see whether he could make his robot turn in a circle, to the surprise of his teacher he came up with the number 360 (his teacher had been expecting him to say '4 lots of 90').

Our experience in using controllable floor robots in the early years is that children talk and listen, revise and review and evaluate and refine the use of their mathematical language in order to be understood and to achieve their joint goals. Mills and Mills (1997: 25) write, 'While elsewhere primacy is given to developing confidence and precision in spoken language, teaching in Britain is dominated by reading, writing and recorded arithmetic'. Many early years mathematical programmes fall into this category of recorded arithmetic and need to be balanced by mathematical experience which is why we place so much emphasis on controllable robots.

One example may demonstrate the learning that can take place with a robot. When working with a class of 6-year-olds I was asked by a substitute teacher to take an extra pupil with my usual group. We were having 'races' with the robot, a race to be the one who could exactly reach a line. There were two robots and the children needed to get to the line by a series of moves based on their estimations of the distance and of the measures in the robot program. The aim was to progress from making a disjointed series of moves to making a single move that would be exact. The new pupil seemed to have worked out that if he added the numbers of the separate moves he could arrive at a total for the complete move. The children were counting out loud to reinforce number and counting for measurement. The new pupil went to the classroom and got a paper and pencil. He asked the other children for the numbers, repeated them and wrote them down. Soon he was suggesting numbers and wanting to do all the inputting as well but when the final race came he was persuaded to take turns.

After the session I returned to the class teacher to tell her of the new pupil's initiative. She asked to see the notebook and congratulated him and then told me that he had arrived that week and spoke no English at all. He had certainly learned his English words for numbers in that session! And I had realised what a nearly universal set of symbols the Arabic numerals are.

Summary

Of all the resources available to early years educationalists at the beginning of the twenty-first century the computer probably inspires the most curiosity and respect from young children.

Though it is as visual as television, engagement with the computer is not passive. A link with the world beyond school, the computer's presence in the classroom reflects the seriousness with which the school regards their education. It offers access to learning for children who are unable to profit from more convergent traditional teaching and it holds out the promise, for all children, that their education is relevant and is concerned with the life that they will engage with as adults. If this promise is to result in educational gains the use of the computer must be more than instrumental. The narrow interpretation of the computer as a tool does not help early years teachers to set aims for themselves other than the oft repeated 'mouse control'.

We have tried to show how the computer can be used for personal exploration and discovery but also we insist that the exposition of the software and the exploration of its potential must be conducted with an adult whose aims include the development of creativity. The most powerful tools at this age are the paint program and the robot. Also exciting are the programs and CD-ROMs which allow the children to explore pattern and story. As with picture books the teacher makes the selection and introduces them to the class, otherwise the potential of powerful and expensive materials is not realised.

Throughout this chapter we have emphasised how various software applications can offer an exciting and imaginative context for learning through play and exploration. Cook and Finlayson (1999) also focus on the importance of play in their book, *Interactive Children, Communicative Teaching*. In the chapter 'Taking play seriously' they quote Labbo's study of kindergarten pupils which highlighted 'the social and personal empowerment through the elevated status they achieved when they became proficient with particular software effects' (Cook and Finlayson 1999: 34).

In many countries in Europe, play is acknowledged as a significant aspect of young children's learning. In England the official Government document, published in 1996, 'for people who work with children of pre-compulsory school age', omitted any mention of play (SCAA 1996). The *Early Learning Goals* (DfEE 1999) has replaced the former document and it includes 180 words on 'play'. There is now an acknowledgement that through play children can 'practise and build up ideas, concepts and skills' (DfEE 1999: 12). We hope that such assertions indicate that at last English educational policy makers are beginning to listen to early years experts in the field.

We have emphasised that the computer is not just a form of transmission but implicit in the design and content of the software are messages about the culture being transmitted. There is not just one style for the computer, a sort of Muppets meets Disney. There is the possibility of employing artistic variety and literary quality which is desirable, because of the way young children revisit material until it has become part of their 'unconscious intelligence' (Claxton 1998). More than anything children need a multiplicity of stimuli and that means a full range of material and resources.

Bruner's twin guides to children's learning apply to the computer as well as to other home and school activity. Adult explication and thoughtful revisiting will enlarge children's understanding and so encourage playful exploration. The computer should not be a lonely tool, a counter-culture of speed and light, divorced from adult input.

Notes

1 The early computers often had a black background to the screen display; the graphics were of a reasonable size and clear enough to be seen by a large group. In the eighties and early nineties teachers taught with these machines to whole groups. Screen presentation of the Windows-type with its black on white imitation of the printed page, is much less clear as there are larger areas of light and the brightness dazzles out the detail of print. This stricture applies also to the now ubiquitous whiteboards as against their antecedent blackboards.
2 The teacher will be aware that the angle in this 'physical geometry' is the angle of turn not the internal angle of Euclidian geometry. Ultimately there is no conflict as they both refer to the circle and children adapt to the different approaches if they are explained.

References

Bruner, J. (1996) What we have learnt about early learning, *The European Early Childhood Education Research Journal*, 4(1).
Claxton, G. (1998) *Hare Brain, Tortoise Mind: Why Intelligence Increases When You Think Less*. London: Fourth Estate.
Cook, D. and Finlayson, H. (1999) *Interactive Children, Communicative Teaching*. Buckingham: Open University Press.
Cox, R. (2000) *Promoting Learning through CD-ROM Talking Books in the Early Years and the Primary School*. Submission for Masters award, University of Kingston.
Crook, C. (1994) *Computers and the Collaborative Experience of Learning*. London: Routledge.
Crook, C. (1998) in K. Littleton and P. Light (eds) *Learning with Computers: Analysing Productive Interaction*. Quoted by B. Lewis (1999) *Book Reviews, JCAL*, 15: 332–4.
DfEE (1999) *Early Learning Goals*. London: QCA Publications.
DfEE (2000) *Curriculum Guidance for the Foundation Stage QCA Publications*. London: QCA Publications.
Fine, C. and Thornbury, M.L. (2000) Children in control, in M. Monteith (ed.) *IT for Learning Enhancement*. Exeter: Intellect Books.
Hopper, M. and Lawler, R.W. (1997) Headstart progress report, in R.W. Lawler (ed.) *Learning with Computers*. Exeter: Intellect Books.
Labbo, L.D. (1996) A semiotic analysis of young children's symbol making in a classroom computer centre, *Reading Research Quarterly*, 51(1): 356–85.
Medwell, J. (1998) The talking books project: Some further insights into the use of talking books to develop reading, *Reading*, 32(1): 3–8.
Meek, M. (1982) What counts as evidence in theories of children's literature? *Theory into Practice*, 21(4): 284–92. Reprinted in P. Hunt (ed.) (1990) *Children's Literature: The Development of Criticism*. London: Routledge.
Mills, C. and Mills, D. (1997) *Britain's Early Years Disaster Part One: The Findings*. Notes supporting Channel Four programme of the same name.
Moseley, D., Higgins, S. et al. (1999) Developing counting skills in reception using ICT, *Ways Forward with ICT*. Newcastle: University of Newcastle.

Papert, S. (1980) *Mindstorms: Children, Computers and Powerful Ideas*. London: Harvester Press.
Papert, S. (1993) *The Children's Machine*. London: Harvester Press.
Postman N. (1993) *Technopoly: The Surrender of Culture to Technology*. New York: Vintage Books.
SCAA (School Curriculum and Assessment Authority) (1996) *Nursery Education: Desirable Outcomes for Children's Learning*. London: Department for Education and Employment.

3
LITERACY AND ICT IN THE EARLY YEARS

Tim Waller

Introduction

This chapter reviews recent research concerning early literacy and ICT. Reference is made to a range of studies from the UK, the USA, Europe, Australia and New Zealand in order to present an international perspective. The chapter also considers what teachers can learn from children's play experiences with new digital technology. In particular, the nature and context of teacher–child interaction during literacy teaching with ICT is examined.

Literacy is an area of learning that the use of ICT could greatly enhance. Moreover, the development of digital technologies has changed the nature of print based literacy and led to the recognition of multiple literacies (Marsh 2004). As Leu (2000) argues, current conceptions of literacy are not adequate when exposed to the light of technological advances such as online and networked ICT, which require us to redefine our understanding of the literacy curriculum. In addition, there is a growing recognition of the impact of digital technology on childhood and children's lives and the need to take account of the child's perspective of electronic media (Yelland 1999).

Traditional activities can now be complemented with different experiences that have been made possible with the new digital and online technologies. These technologies, and the activities that children may engage in with them, have the potential to extend learning in new and exciting ways. Currently however, in some curriculum frameworks, the potential of ICT is not recognised and traditional conceptions of literacy seem to overwhelm the new, emerging conceptions of literacy.

New technology such as 'talking books', multimedia and 'talking word processors' could allow children far more independence from the teacher in literacy tasks and free the teacher to focus teaching on the distinctive features of reading and the written process. In addition, the use of digital cameras and multimedia composing tools has the potential to transform children's storytelling and writing. The combination of image, sound and text could engage young children to attend to textual features and provide support for emergent literacy. Further, images include details and nuances that are more difficult for beginning readers to glean from text. Visual images can also serve as a focal point for shared discussion, and assist children to develop their ideas in a socially mediated context.

This chapter discusses research and evidence that demonstrates how ICT can be integrated into teaching and learning to transform literacy practice in the early years. It will be argued that learning to be literate involves developing an understanding and familiarity with electronic literacies; this is a necessary accomplishment for both children and teachers.

The context of early literacy and ICT

Many countries throughout the world have recently made significant investment in educational ICT. In the UK, for example, the government has spent in excess of £2 billion on ICT kit for schools and in 'training' teachers to use the technology. Children and teachers are now clearly expected to function and develop within an online community and network, while (in the UK) schools are appraised, judged, measured and regulated through a series of online reports, league tables and data available to those with access to the Internet. As we move from 'e-learning' (electronic learning) to 'm-learning' (mobile learning), using small multifunction devices and out of the computer suite and into the classroom (not before time), there is a need to comprehend the accelerating technological change in our daily educational and working lives.

One important question is how these initiatives combine so that the potential of ICT is fully utilised to support young children's emerging literacy. McFarlane (1997) has cautioned against curriculum models being far removed from 'authentic' learning. She argues that a literacy curriculum should respect and respond to children's own ideas and perceptions. Godwin and Perkins (1998) and Marsh and Hallet (1999) also have reservations about curriculum frameworks that are imposed and prescribed by central government. As Dombey (1998: 41) points out, learning literacy in the early years is very complex. She suggests that adequate consideration needs to be given to factors that move children into literacy and the changing nature of literacy as ICT influences practice. Recently there have been a plethora of online sources promoting the use ICT in literacy teaching and learning. The limitation of some of these resources is that they are mainly focused on a narrow print based view of literacy and are for older children. Goodwyn et al. (1997) and Marsh and Hallet (1999) and Marsh (2004) advocate an approach which considers a far more complex and broadly conceived model of literacy that recognises the many varied practices involved in meaning making and includes the spoken word and written and visual text. Further, along with Whitehead (1999), the emphasis is on literacy practices that are located within a meaningful context where purpose is the prime consideration.

It can be argued that there are considerable benefits for learning when using ICT to promote literacy. These benefits can be realised within the literacy curriculum and at other times. Despite the recent increased funding of ICT resources in schools however, there are still some major issues concerning teacher's experience of ICT, access, curriculum application, management and resources that are hindering the realisation of this potential. Access remains a critical issue. For example, there is a tendency to assume that World Wide Web means that the whole world is connected to the Internet but approximately 96 per cent of the world's population is not. There are clear divisions based on class, 'race', gender, age and geography, both within the UK and the rest of the world. As children from affluent socio-economic backgrounds usually have greater access to new technology it becomes vital that schools equip children, at all levels, with the appropriate ICT skills and experience (Waller 2004). For Rivalland (2000), the challenge for governments, policy writers and educators is to resource schools in such a way that powerful forms of electronic literacy can be made available to all children, most particularly those children who are already marked with the inequities of poverty, illness and other forms of social inequity. She asserts that:

> No longer can any of us who are involved with childcare, pre-schools or schools be excused for blaming the homes and parents of these children, because such children make up a large sector of our population. Finding ways of connecting to the interests and literate practices of these children is an essential part of the early literacy work to be done by all of us who work with children.
>
> (Rivalland 2000: 8)

Some early years educators, however, are very sceptical about the benefits of young children's use of computers. Healy (1999) raises concerns that ICT will cause harm to children's development because computers may replace traditional play activities and increase the possibility that they become social isolates. This view is not in accordance with almost all of the published writing on ICT but it does remind us that not all adults working with young children are advocates for technology.

Baker (2000) and Waller (2000) argue that early years teachers have a significant responsibility to foster children's abilities to read and write and currently they are also encouraged to incorporate technology in their classrooms. Waller (2000) asserts that there is a strong justification for using ICT in early literacy activities. First, ICT is a tool that many children are familiar with. Second, ICT may help to provide the motivation for some children who find reading and writing difficult. In addition, there is a growing body of research evidence that demonstrates benefits of ICT for teaching and learning (as discussed later in the chapter). Further, it is no longer enough to teach children to read traditional texts. They need to become familiar with the range of texts that are significant in adult life today, including screen and web based texts. However, although new technology has now become commonplace in early childhood classrooms, many early years educators are unsure how to make the best use of the technology – the recent introduction of electronic whiteboards into many early years classrooms is an example. Also, teachers wonder how to design computer activities to meet the individual needs of children at various levels of literacy (Labbo et al. 2000).

New technology, play and early literacy

While relatively little research has been undertaken with young children under 8 years of age using new technology in general, there is a growing recognition of the impact of ICT on children's lives, particularly from the USA (Labbo et al. 2000), Australia (Luke 1999; Yelland 1999) and the UK (Facer et al. 2003; Marsh 2004), for example. They put forward the view that electronic media has a significant influence on childhood and suggest that children's early literacy and play experiences are shaped increasingly by electronic media.

O'Hara (2004) discusses the role of ICT in supporting play in a number of early years settings in England. In terms of imaginative role-play opportunities, fully functional ICT was used and controlled by the children to support emergent literacy in 'offices', 'travel agents' and 'cafes', etc. Here the ICT can enable a 'print-rich' environment. Van Scoter and Boss (2002) also suggest using computers and printers to help children make signs, banners and other props for pretend play.

The potential of computer games to support learning has been a contentious issue in the media but has been recently recognised within the literature (Yelland 2002). Verenikina et al. (2003) argue that for many children computer games are a significant part of their daily experiences and that early years practitioners need to understand how the games impact on the children's lives. Bolstad (2004) has developed a useful table for assessing the contribution of computer games to children's play.

As ICT becomes established in the classroom it is also important that teachers learn about the effect of its influence on children's learning. Yelland (1999) has raised the significant issue of the need to consider the nature of impact of digital technology on childhood and takes account of the child's perspective of electronic media. Yelland (1999) points out that developments in technology have moved with extreme speed over the past few years and argues that there is a need to consider new definitions of what it means to play with both physical objects and digital ones. She contends that traditional activities can now be complemented with different experiences that have been made possible with the new information and communications technologies. For Yelland, these technologies, and the activities that children may engage in with them, have the potential to extend learning in new and exciting ways: 'As early childhood educators, we need to be aware of the potential of such environments as contexts for play. In this way, we can facilitate the learning process and help children to make sense of their world in ways that were not possible up to this time' (Yelland 1999: 220). She considers the impact of the new information technologies on play and *as* play. She suggests that ICT has the potential not only to enhance learning, but also to promote engagement with ideas in new and dynamic ways. For example, the availability of digital toys which enable the child to engage in fantasy contexts as well as to create interactions which have personal significance.

Luke (1999) and Yelland (1999) etc., therefore, present an argument that the use of digital play opportunities can strengthen everyday literacy teaching and learning in early childhood classrooms. However, as Dombey (1998, 1999) and Roskos and Hanbali (2000) point out, there is a concern among early childhood educators that the important role of play in the process of learning to read and write might be misunderstood, if not overlooked altogether. They argue that the current reality of early literacy practice is that it involves intensely instructive activities that are seen as best led by adults who impart essential literacy knowledge and skills that children must learn: 'After all, children need to develop phonemic awareness, learn letter names, practice recognizing words, and participate actively in storybook reading to acquire basic literacy concepts. Certainly this is serious business, and the time and energy it demands can overwhelm thoughts of play' (Roskos and Hanbali 2000: 1).

Long-established play and literacy activities in early years classrooms can now be complemented with different experiences that have been made possible with the new information technologies. These technologies, and the activities that children may engage in with them, have the potential to extend learning in new and exciting ways and strengthen everyday literacy teaching and learning in early childhood classrooms. In this context learning is not only fun but children actively construct their own meaning and make sense of the world in their own ways. It is in direct contrast to much of the current literacy practice, where the learner is often passive and the teacher acts as the conductor of content and actions. If the potential of ICT is not exploited in this way it seems that there is a possibility of a mismatch between the learning process of children and teaching methods (Yelland 1999).

There are therefore two problems faced by early years teachers: first, maintaining an appropriate literacy curriculum that includes suitable opportunities for play and, second including activities that allow children to draw on their experiences of digital technology in their play.

Bilingual and multilingual children, literacy and ICT

It is argued that the needs of young bilingual and multilingual learners are not always fully recognised in literacy frameworks. Gregory (1996) and Minns (1997) draw attention to the cultural mismatch that can occur between home and school literacy experiences, which can disadvantage emergent bilingual readers and writers. However, there are possibilities for new technology to support children from culturally or linguistically diverse backgrounds. Castellani and Tsantis (2002) suggest that the use of appropriate software can allow children to engage in self-exploration and meet their individual needs in a way that traditional print-based material is unable to match, thus, affording teachers opportunities to structure the learning environment in culturally inclusive ways.

Gregory (1996) showed that opportunities to explicitly build on the rhythms and patterns of spoken language are especially beneficial with bilingual children. Castellani and Tsantis (2002) discuss a project, based in the USA, where bilingual children were given regular access to software that explored basic concepts such as colour, numbers and shapes in their native language, as well as offering the English language equivalent of these concepts. Brooker and Siraj-Blatchford (2002) reported the experiences of three and four year-old bilingual children who were at an early stage of English acquisition, in an urban nursery school. They argued that the children's language around the computer was clearly supported by the 'structured but accessible format and vocabulary of the software' (2002: 263). For example, the researchers regularly noted instances of language learning, and children repeating words and phrases in response to computer-spoken prompts. For Brooker and Siraj-Blatchford, computer use by bilingual children is therefore seen as 'especially valuable'. They point out that: 'The computer often provided a shared focus and experience for children who didn't share the same spoken language, and this undoubtedly contributed towards the development of the very positive, collaborative, and language enriched multicultural learning environment that we observed' (Brooker and Siraj-Blatchford 2002: 269).

Bolstad (2004) discusses a number of examples of ICT used to support early literacy in both English and Maori in New Zealand. Several early childhood centres have used ICT to produce multimedia learning stories co-authored between children, educators and, sometimes, parents (Lee et al. 2002; Wilson et al. 2003).

Also, Ferguson and Mellow (2004) describe a resource, available online and as a CD-ROM, which they developed to support young children's development of Maori. The resource includes a number of activities that use a mixture of images, recorded sounds, numbers, written words and letters, with mouse-based drag-and-drop and roll-over interactions. Practitioners are encouraged to work through activities with children, and to read out positive reinforcement messages in English and Maori.

Van Scoter and Boss (2002) describe an early years setting in Oregon where teachers often send home digital photos of children's activities and out of school visits. Working with children to put captions on these photos offers an opportunity to develop children's written language skills as children use their own words to describe what the photos show. This strategy is considered a particularly useful one to support children's oral language development in their native language. Shepherd (2002) reports on a project in Scotland involving the creation of software to support the transition from home to nursery, particularly for children whose first language is not English. A digital camera was used to take photographs of children following nursery routines. 'Clicker' software was used to present these, together with spoken commentary in English and other relevant languages.

The above examples demonstrate that new technology has significant potential to support young bilingual learners, but much further research in this area is a priority for informing practice in the early years.

New technology and emergent literacies

The development and use of communication technologies has far outpaced research on computer-mediated literacy (Reinking et al. 2000). Most studies of emergent literacy focus on print-based literacy which can lead to an overemphasis on the formal skills of reading and writing print. Marsh (2004) argues that early literacy is in transition and that the dynamic and complex nature of contemporary childhood literacy practices should be acknowledged. Leu (2000) also suggests that the appearance in our classrooms of networked ICT, such as the Internet, requires us to redefine our understanding of the literacy curriculum. As a result Marsh (2004: 4) argues that the plural form, 'literacies' has become widely adopted to acknowledge the range of literacy and communicative practices developed through computers, television and mobile phones.

Gamble and Easingwood (2000) explore how the potential of new technologies can be exploited in a way that advances the definition of literacy and Brindley (2000) contrasts the narrow, individual and text-based definition of school literacy with a much more dynamic model that recognises learning through a range of media, including hypertext, video, graphics and sound. In this broader view human interaction with technology is recognised and literacy is seen as a much more collaborative process, with participants communicating through electronic networks in emerging online communities. Rivalland (2000) also argues for a concept of literacy that recognises the possibilities for children who will grow up in what she calls a 'multimodal world'. She advocates the teaching of: 'a literacy which encourages children to be aware of the values in all texts; a literacy which recognizes that technology can reshape the social relations of doing literacy . . . and which will provide children with the social capital and critical awareness to make use of these texts within appropriate contexts.' (Rivalland 2000: 1).

Lankshear and Knobel (2003) reviewed international research concerning new technology and early childhood literacy. They found a very limited number of articles in mainstream literacy journals concerning new technology and literacy and, almost none concerning early literacy. In general, literacy was treated in a non-dynamic way and that the overwhelming emphasis on how technology was used to support traditional alphabetic and print-based literacy. While there has been a lack of school based multimodal research, there is also little research on new technology and literacies out of school. Marsh (2004) argues that the emergent techno-literacies of young children should be more widely acknowledged. These include the narratives influenced and developed by TV, computer games and mobile phones.

As Topping and McKenna (1999) point out, for those with access, the potential for flow of worldwide information direct into the home is enormous. There are two possible developments: first, schools can support and promote the development of electronic literacy in the home; and second electronic literacy activities can develop independently in the home irrespective of any school involvement. The integration of electronic literacy with family literacy has been termed 'family electronic literacy' (Topping 1997; Topping et al. 1997). The aims are similar to those for family literacy, but set in an electronic environment. Electronic literacy refers to literacy activities (e.g. in reading, writing and spelling) that are delivered, supported, accessed or assessed digitally through computers or other electronic means rather than on paper. Topping and McKenna (1999) discuss electronic literacy as a selection of activities that are digitally accessed through computers. They offer a typology of electronic literacy and suggest that current developments in computer-based electronic literacy can be considered in a number of categories:

1. Electronically supported reading;
2. Electronically supported writing;
3. Electronic audiences;
4. Electronic literacy assessment, feedback and management; and
5. Electronic direct speech-text conversion.

In addition to literacy gains, participants might develop some transferable skills in the use of ICT. The effectiveness of these more recent developments has been less well documented as yet, although some early indications are encouraging. Labbo and Watkins (1996) report on a successful programme, involving kindergarten children taking laptop computers home to produce pictorial responses to literature using a computer drawing package. In the UK the Dockland's Learning Acceleration Project (Barker et al. 2000) involved children and families at home in the effective use of hand-held pocket book computers to develop story writing.

The project studied 600 seven and eight year-olds in school and at home. Results from the project suggest that using multimedia and portable technology, as well as more traditional methods, could raise the levels and expectations of children's literacy.

New technology and print-based literacy

While there has been far more published research on the use of ICT with older primary children, there is an increasing body of work giving examples of effective use with young children (from two to eight years). Cohen (1997) reported on long-term projects in France which have investigated the use of ICT to support the development of children's written language from the ages of three to ten. For Cohen these projects demonstrated the following possible benefits of the use of ICT in young children's literacy learning:

- greater motivation to become involved in written language;
- an earlier self sufficiency (particularly since the advent of speech feedback software).

Eisenwine and Hunt (2000) discuss a project that involved using a computer in literacy groups with emergent readers. They argued that children made 'significant gains' not only in emergent literacy behaviours, including communication, but also in positive interactions.

Medrano and Nivela (1997) show how the development of a computer corner in a nursery school could help to foster interaction and co-operation among peers and promote literacy development. They aimed to integrate the computer corner into the 'dynamics of the classroom' (1997:

51). In terms of literacy, they suggest that the use of the computer corner led to improvements in spatiality and letter recognition but they did not advance a detailed explanation of how the computer supported these developments. Labbo et al. (2000) engaged in ethnographic research into young children's opportunities for literacy development in a kindergarten classroom through the use of a computer centre. They observed that many children with low literacy abilities were not benefiting from interacting with programs designed to provide them with practice on literacy skills (e.g. alphabetic order, letter identification, sound-symbol relationships). Following on from these observations, they proposed that involving children in brief, highly focused activities at the computer centre, could be beneficial to their literacy development (2000: 9). As a result of their research Labbo et al. recommend that the most effective use of ICT to support literacy is when the teacher finds a way to use the technology to support children's literacy needs and to enhance the thematic units and literature based activities occurring in the classroom.

ICT and learning to read

There is a developing body of research evidence indicating that ICT will help children learn to read if used in the right way. Medwell (1998), Lewin (2000) and Underwood (2000) examined the use of 'talking books'. They suggested that using talking stories increases children's word reading accuracy, both in the context of the story and out of context; improves children's understanding of the stories and supports children's reading by offering them access to the meaning of the stories and the way sentences work. They also point out that these programs are more effective for boys who seemed to show greater increases in word accuracy than girls when using talking stories. Collins et al. (1997) believe that talking books are not only accessible and highly motivating but also: 'have the potential to develop reading skills by giving children the overview of the story prior to reading it, by supporting children's independent reading through sounding out unrecognized words and by encouraging collaborative reading in front of a public "page" ' (Collins et al. 1997: 34).

Further, Medwell (1998) argues that the use of this particular type of software offers the following benefits for young readers:

- giving children the overview of the story prior to reading it;
- supporting children's independent reading through sounding out unrecognised words;
- making the features of narrative explicit;
- encouraging collaborative reading in front of a public 'page'.

The combination of speech and text has, therefore, the potential to support children's reading. Medwell (1996) found that when children explored the talking stories prior to reading with the teacher, there was a significant increase in word accuracy. Moseley et al. (1999: ix) suggest that a clear progression is identified by the literature. Beginning readers are helped by the addition of speech for word recognition (e.g. talking books). Speech support then assists with writing and spelling by encouraging children to re-read (or have the computer read) their work to identify where improvement was possible. More fluent readers are encouraged to extend their reading comprehension through the spoken support for new words and the availability of a spoken dictionary. Moseley et al. (1999: ix) also review illustrations of 'effective pedagogy with ICT' and assert that the children involved 'made significant progress over a term in reading age, word recognition and spelling age'.

However, more recent research has suggested that early years practitioners need to discriminate between useful and less useful types of talking story. Labbo and Kuhn (1998) classified talking books in terms of 'considerate' (where animations are used to support the story) and 'inconsiderate' (where animations are illogical and disrupt the telling of the print-based story). De Jong and Bus (2003), in their investigation of electronic storybooks, also found the most useful CD-ROMs combined multimedia with interactive additions that actually supported literacy within the story.

Collaboration, writing and ICT

A significant body of research conducted in the USA has been concerned with investigating aspects of the integration of literacy instruction and technology (e.g. Reinking et al. 1998; Daiute 2000; Leu 2000). One area of this research examines the impact of word processors on written expression. Most studies have shown word processors to be beneficial. However, there is still only limited research evidence to support this assertion in terms of early writers. New technology offers a variety of ways for emergent readers and writers to combine words and pictures. Van Scoter and Boss (2002) discuss the benefits of digital photography. Working with children to put captions on photos they have taken offers an opportunity to develop children's written language skills, while photos with captions deliberately left off can promote children's oral language skills, as children use their own words to describe what the photos show. There are many ways in which ICT can support children's storytelling. As Van Scoter and Boss (2002) have shown, young children could dictate words to go with their pictures or they could record their voices telling the story or be videotaped as they tell the story and show the picture.

For more experienced writers, studies indicate that word processors can help children to focus on the content they are writing about, increase cohesion, promote metacognitive talk, increase collaboration and active involvement among children (Baker 2000). Research that focuses on the impact of the Internet and electronic communication on development of writing suggests that through Internet technology writers increase their awareness of their audience and gain useful feedback (Leu 2000).

The computer, because of the public nature of the screen, can become a natural focus for interaction and collaboration among writers. For Daiute (2000) collaborative writing with a partner involves children in composing processes that make explicit the social nature of writing. Children engage in a range of playful and metacognitive strategies when composing with peers. She asserts that 'collaborative writing is a socially embedded use of word processors' (2000: 1). As tools that allow writers to merge and revise ideas in text, word processors can be integral to creative and critical composing. The benefit of the word processor is that individual contributions can be merged into one via typing, merging and editing facilities. The collaboration is, thus, embodied in the word processed text. Furthermore, Daiute has argued that peer collaborative writing on the computer has been associated with greater improvement than has writing with only the teacher.

There is also a use for word processors to support the shared writing of narrative texts. Shared writing is where the teacher works with a group to compose stories and acts as the scribe to discuss and model the writing process. Scrimshaw (1993) also emphasised the particular contribution that ICT can make to collaborative writing by facilitating brainstorming, composing, conferencing and publication. When composing with a partner, children have the benefit of experiencing the role of writer and reader as they respond to a partner's suggestion of specific text sequences and listen to a partner's reactions (Daiute 2000: 7). This approach fosters collaboration by providing young authors with opportunities to share their writing, at which time they receive feedback and together explore the reading–writing connection.

Scaffolding literacy and ICT

Waller (2002) carried out research focused on the use of ICT to support early literacy. In particular, the project was concerned with investigating the role of the teacher in literacy teaching and learning with ICT. Reference was made to Wray and Medwell's (1998) four-stage model of the teaching process: demonstration, joint activity, supported activity and individual activity. Waller undertook a detailed analysis of the 'joint activity' between children and teachers, through videotape and observations. Joint activity was defined by the following characteristics: proximity, time, style and attention. The study was carried out with 24 teachers and their primary or nursery school classes with children aged three to eight years, over a period of two years.

LITERACY AND ICT IN THE EARLY YEARS

The evidence collected and examined during this project suggests that ICT has not had a significant impact on literacy learning in the early years classrooms investigated. Relatively little evidence of any 'joint activity' or 'scaffolding' was actually observed or recorded, except in nursery and reception classes (see Figure 3.1). Generally, teachers tended to instruct children in the use of a program, they sometimes used ICT for demonstration and then they tended to leave children to work on computers independently, unless a technical problem occurred. The focus of the teacher's language and interaction tended to revolve around management of technical matters concerning the functioning of the ICT tool, such as printing. During the 24 observed sessions ICT was used mainly for individual activity in the teaching and learning of literacy.

Figure 3.1 shows the frequency of observed interaction for literacy and ICT. It is noticeable that joint activity was significantly higher in nursery and reception classes (42) (age five) and individual activity is much higher in classes from age six to eight especially at age eight. Nursery and reception teachers spent 36 per cent of the observed time engaged in joint activity and 28 per cent of the time supporting children. Demonstration and individual activity were equally distributed at 18 per cent. By comparison, the teachers of the older children spent 20 per cent of their time

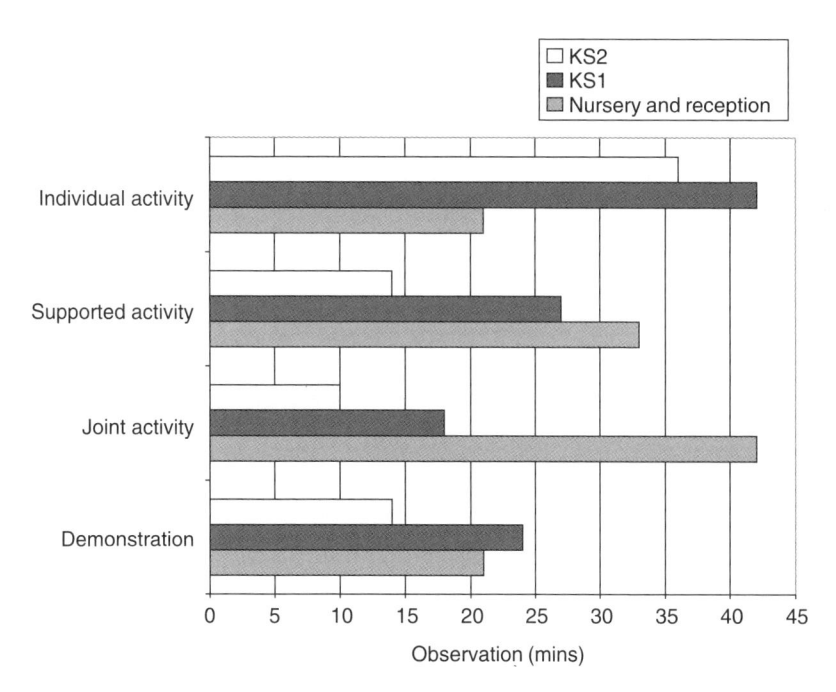

Figure 3.1 Frequency of observed interaction (by type)

in demonstration, 15 per cent on joint activity and 22 per cent supporting children's learning.

Waller also found a noticeable difference in time and style of interaction between nursery and reception teachers and those in classrooms for older children, categorised as 'age specific teaching style'. A feature of age specific teaching style was that the nursery and reception teachers spent much more time engaged in joint activity with the children. The older children's teachers' practices, however, were subject to and influenced by their curriculum and the National Literacy Strategy. In the older children's classrooms it was observed that ICT was found to be used mainly for independent activity by children.

As with Facer et al. (2003), Waller found that many children feel that they have IT skills and that they gain them outside school. There is therefore a strong argument that the role of the teacher changes as a result of the introduction of ICT into the classroom. This new role includes providing opportunities and contexts to exploit the potential of children's experience of electronic literacies in the wider community.

Teachers need to know their children's capabilities and interests to understand how to organise their classroom and to structure the teaching of their children so that ICT resources become an integral part of the learning.

Conclusion

This chapter has discussed examples of the effective use of ICT for teaching and learning early literacy. Much of the recent research would seem to confirm that ICT could enhance young children's reading and writing, particularly when the technology used includes a speech feedback facility such as a 'talking word processor'. However, most literature relates to a narrow print based view of literacy and there is a need for much further research involving digital literacies. There is evidence that many teachers are generally positive about ICT and have a conception that computers should be of value to them and their children, but they are underestimating children's experience and confidence with ICT and are unwilling to take risks with their classroom practice (Waller 2002).

The role of the teacher in guiding and assisting children's learning with ICT is therefore seen as critical, both for literacy and other areas of learning. This chapter has argued that teachers have an important role in supporting early literacy through joint activity around a computer. This joint activity is characterised by reciprocity that acknowledges the child's experience and confidence with ICT at home and leads to assisted performance that is recognised by the child. Further, it is clear that simply placing new technologies in our classrooms will not prepare children adequately for the new literacies they require, they have to be integrated effectively into classroom practice. Access and equity are significant issues in the use of ICT for promoting and supporting literacy, although paradoxically the technology can help increase access through libraries and family electronic literacy projects. The critical issue about technology and young children is not *if* it should be used but *how* it is best used to enhance their (literacy) development. Tharp and Gallimore argue that: 'Emerging instructional practices provide some hope for increased use of assisted performance; the increase of small groups, maintenance of positive classroom atmosphere that will increase independent task involvement of students, new materials and technology which students can act independent of the teacher' (Tharp and Gallimore 1998: 107).

However, while this view of the potential of ICT to enhance classroom learning is attractive, it is contended here that there is a need to take into account the wider political, social and cultural context of literacy and ICT, including children's experience of digital play, so as to fully understand the nature of classroom learning and interaction. It is the teachers, as Leu (2000) points out, *and* the children who are experienced at using the Internet in their classrooms and homes who are likely to provide us with an important direction. The instructional strategies, interaction and resources, tested in the classroom and at home need to be further articulated and clarified to resolve the challenge of achieving the real potential of ICT to support the teaching and learning of literacy.

Appendix

Useful online sources for early literacy and ICT:

- http://www.ltscotland.org.uk/earlyyears/
  Learning and Teaching in Scotland. A very good site for ICT and early years in general.
- http://www.ioe.stir.ac.uk/Interplay/
  Interplay Project – Play learning and ICT in the Foundation Stage.
- http://www.camelsdale.w-sussex.sch.uk/
  Camelsdale First School site. Examples of early years and ICT and resources.
- http://www.hitchams.suffolk.sch.uk/foundation/
  Sir Robert Hitcham's Primary School site. Examples of early years and ICT and resources.
- http://www.kidsmartearlylearning.org/EN/
  Activities and links for home and school.
- http://www.teem.org.uk/
  Software reviews.

References

Baker, E.A. (2000) Instructional approaches used to integrate literacy and technology, *Reading Online*, 4(1). Available at http://www.readingonline.org/articles/baker/ (accessed 1 August 2000).
Barker, R., Franklin, G. and Meadows, J. (2000) Reading, writing and ICT, in R. Bolstad (ed.) (2004) *The Role and Potential of ICT in Early Childhood Education*. New Zealand: Ministry of Education.
Bolstad, R. (2004) *The Role and Potential of ICT in Early Childhood Education*. New Zealand: Ministry of Education.
Brindley, S. (2000) ICT and literacy, in N. Gamble and N. Easingwood (eds) *ICT and Literacy*. London: Continuum.
Brooker, L. and Siraj-Blatchford, J. (2002) 'Click on miaow!': How children of three and four years experience the nursery computer, *Contemporary Issues in Early Childhood: Technology Special Issue*, 3(2): 251–73.
Castellani, J. and Tsantis, L. (2002) Cross-cultural reactions to using computers in the early childhood education classroom, *Contemporary Issues in Early Childhood: Technology Special Issue*, 3(2): 274–88.
Cohen, R.D. (1997) The discovery of written language in the computer age, in J.M. Collins, M. Hammond and J. Wellington (eds) (1997) *Teaching and Learning with Multimedia*. London: Routledge.
Daiute, C. (2000) Writing and communication technologies, in R. Indrisano and J.R. Squire (eds) Perspectives on Writing: Research, Theory, and Practice, *Reading Online*. Available at www.readingonline.org (Posted May 2000, accessed 1 August 2000).
De Jong, M. and Bus, A.G. (2003) How well suited are electronic books to supporting literacy? *Journal of Early Childhood Literacy*, 3(2): 147–64.
Dombey, H. (1998) A totalitarian approach to literacy education? *Forum*, 20(2): 36–41.
Dombey, H. (1999) Picking a path through the phonics minefield, *Education 3–13*, 27(1): 12–21.
Eisenwine, M.J. and Hunt, D.A. (2000) Using a computer in literacy groups with emergent readers, *Reading Teacher*, 53(6): 456–63.
Facer, K., Furlong, J., Furlong, R. and Sutherland, R. (2003) *ScreenPlay: Children and Computing in the Home*. London: RoutledgeFalmer.
Ferguson, S. and Mellow, P. (2004) *Whakahihiko te Hinengaro*: Lessons from a preschool te reo e-learning resource, *Computers in New Zealand Schools*, 16(2): 41–4.
Gamble, N. and Easingwood, N. (eds) (2000) *ICT and Literacy*. London: Continuum.
Godwin, D. and Perkins, M. (1998) *Teaching Language and Literacy in the Early Years*. London: David Fulton.
Goodwyn, A., Adams, A. and Clarke, S. (1997) The great god of the future: the views of current and future English teachers on the place of IT in literacy English, *Education 3–13*, 31(2): 54–62.
Gregory, E. (1996) *Making Sense of a New World: Learning to Read in a Second Language*. London: Paul Chapman Publishing.
Healy, J.M. (1999) *Failure to Connect*. London: Simon and Schuster.
Labbo, L.D. and Kuhn, M. (1998) Computers and emergent literacy: An examination of young children's computer generated communicative symbol making, in D.R. Reinking, L.D. Labbo, M. McKenna and R. Keiffer (eds) *Literacy*

for the 21st Century: Technological Transformations in a Post-Typographic World. Mahwah, NJ: Erlbaum.

Labbo, L.D., Sprague, L., Montero, M.K. and Font, G. (2000) Connecting a computer center to themes, literature, and kindergartners' literacy needs, *Reading Online*, 4(1). Available at http://www.readingonline.org/electronic/labbo/ (accessed 6 August 2000).

Labbo, L. and Watkins, J. (1996) Screenland: Kindergartners stances toward computer-generated responses to literature. Paper presented at the 41st International Reading Association Annual Convention, New Orleans, L.A., April.

Lankshear, C. and Knobel, M. (2003) New technologies in early childhood literacy research: A review of research, *Journal of Early Childhood Literacy*, 3(1): 59–82.

Lee, W., Hatherly, A. and Ramsey, K. (2002) Using ICT to document children's learning, *Early Childhood Folio*, 6: 10–16.

Leu, D. (2000) Our children's future: Changing the focus of literacy and literacy instruction, *Reading Online*. Available at www.readingonline.org (Posted March 2000, accessed 3 May 2000).

Lewin, C. (2000) Exploring the effects of talking book software in UK primary classrooms, *Journal of Research in Reading*, 23(2): 149–57.

Luke, C. (1999) What next? Toddler netizens, playstation thumb, techno-literacies, *Contemporary Issues in Early Childhood*, 1(1): 95–100.

Marsh, J. (2000) Teletubby tales: Popular culture in the early years language and literacy curriculum, *Contemporary Issues in Early Childhood*, 1(2): 119–33.

Marsh, J. (ed.) (2004) *Popular Culture, New Media and Digital Literacy*. London: RoutledgeFalmer.

Marsh, J. and Hallet, E. (1999) *Desirable Literacies*. London: Paul Chapman Publishing.

McFarlane, A. (ed.) (1997) *Information Technology and Authentic Learning*. London: Routledge.

McFarlane, A. (2000) Communicating meaning: Reading and writing in a multimedia world, in N. Gamble and N. Easingwood (eds) *ICT and Literacy*. London: Continuum.

Medrano, G. and Nivela, M.L.H. (1997) A computer corner for three year old children, in J.M. Casey (ed.) *Early Literacy: The Empowerment of Technology*. Englewood, CO: Libraries Unlimited Inc.

Medwell, J. (1996) Talking books and reading, *Reading*, April, 41–6.

Medwell, J. (1998) The talking books project: Some further insights into the use of talking books to develop reading, *Reading*, April, 3–8.

Minns, H. (1997) *Read It To Me Now*. Buckingham: Open University Press.

Moseley, D., Higgins, S., Bramald, R. et al. (1999) *Ways Forward with ICT: Effective Pedagogy Using Information and Communications Technology for Literacy and Numeracy in Primary Schools*. Newcastle: University of Newcastle.

O'Hara, M. (2004) *ICT in the Early Years*. London: Continuum.

Reinking, D., Labbo, L.D. and McKenna, M.C. (2000) From assimilation to accommodation: A developmental framework for integrating digital technologies into literacy research and instruction, *Journal of Research in Reading*, 23(2): 110–22.

Reinking, D., McKenna, M.C., Labbo, L.D. and Kieffer, R.D. (eds) (1998) *Literacy for the 21st Century: Technological Transformations in a Post-Typographical World*. Mahwah, NJ: Erlbaum.

Rivalland, J. (2000) Learning to be literate: So whose responsibility is it? *Darwin Conference Papers*. Available at www.aeca.org.au/ (accessed 20 July 2000).

Roskos, K. and Hanbali, O.M. (2000) Creating connections, building constructions: Language, literacy, and play in early childhood. An invited commentary, *Reading Online*. Available at www.readingonline.org (Posted May 2000, accessed 1 August 2000).

Scrimshaw, P. (1993) *Language, Computers and Classrooms*. London: Routledge.

Shepherd, K. (2002) *A Multi-lingual Introduction to the Nursery*. Available at www.ltscotland.org.uk/ictineducation/innovationawards (Accessed 13 January 2004).

Tharp, R. and Gallimore, R. (1998) A theory of teaching as assisted performance, in D. Faulkener, K. Littleton and M. Woodhead (eds) *Learning Relationships in the Classroom*. London: Routledge.

Topping, K.J. (1997) Family electronic literacy: home–school links through computers *Reading*, 31(2).

Topping, K.J., Bircham, A. and Shaw, M. (1997) Family electronic literacy: home–school links through audiotaped books, *Reading*, 31(2).

Topping, K.J. and McKenna, M.C. (1999) Introduction to electronic literacy, Part Two, *Reading and Writing Quarterly*, 15(3): 193–4.

Underwood, J. (2000) A comparison of two types of computer support for reading development, *Journal of Research in Reading*, 23(2): 136–48.

Van Scoter, J. and Boss, S. (2002) *Learners, Language, and Technology: Making Connections that Support Literacy*, Northwest Regional Educational Laboratory. Available at www.netc.org/earlyconnections/pub/index.html (accessed: 1 August 2004).

Verenikina, I., Harris, P. and Lysaght, P. (2003) Child's play: Computer games, theories of play and children's development. Paper presented at the Young Children and Learning Technologies conference, UWS Parramatta, July.

Waller, T. (2000) Computer Meets Classroom: Children and Teachers Win? *International Journal of Educational Policy, Research and Practice*, 1(3): 337–61.

Waller, T. (2002) Cognition and technology: Scaffolding early literacy through ICT. Paper presented at European Conference on Educational Research, Lisbon, Portugal, September.

Waller, T. (2004) Educational technology, surplus value and the digital divide. Paper presented at the British Educational Research Association Annual Conference, Manchester, September.

Whitehead, M. (1999) *Supporting Language and Literacy Development in the Early Years*. Buckingham: Open University Press.

Wilson, P., Clarke, M., Maley-Shaw, C. and Kelly, M. (2003) 'Smile, you're on digital camera!' Collaboration between communities, children, and computers. *Early Education*, 33: 39–46.

Wray, D. and Medwell, J. (1998) *Teaching English in Primary Schools*. London: Letts.

Yelland, N.J. (1999) Technology as Play, *Early Childhood Education Journal*, 26(4): 217–25.

Yelland, N. (2002). Playing with ideas and games in early mathematics, *Contemporary Issues in Early Childhood: Technology Special Issue*, 3(2): 197–215.

4

MATHEMATICS AND ICT IN THE EARLY YEARS

Richard Bennett

What is the most effective way to help children become numerate – and how might information and communications technology assist in this process? Is the best use being made of computer technology to support the teaching and learning of mathematics in the early years classroom?

This chapter attempts to answer these questions by examining the implications for classroom teaching of current thinking about mathematics education. It relates theoretical underpinning to the role of the computer in teaching and learning and studies the reality of the use of the computer in early years mathematics teaching through the context of the English education system.

First hand mathematics experiences

The value of first hand experience for teaching and learning is firmly rooted in early years practice and has been so for many years: 'Begin where the learner is' (Froebel [1887] 1992). The same is no less true for the teaching and learning of mathematics today. Current understanding of the way children learn mathematical concepts and procedures has been heavily influenced by constructivist theories derived from the work of Piaget, Bruner and Vygotsky.

Children's implicit mathematical knowledge

It has long been accepted that pre-school children possess considerable implicit mathematical knowledge and experience, often to quite sophisticated levels of understanding (Gelman and Gallistel 1978). Hughes (1986) demonstrates that by the age of five most children can carry out a range of additions and subtractions in concrete and hypothetical situations. Many mathematics educators argue for teaching methods which acknowledge and build upon children's individual knowledge and understanding. Liebeck (1984) bases her ELPS (Experience–Language–Pictures–Symbols) approach on the work of Bruner. She suggests that children should encounter mathematical situations initially through first hand experience (Experience) and should be encouraged to discuss what they see and do (Language). This will enable them to internalise their experiences. They should then be supported in representing the situations through drawings which are meaningful to them (Pictures) and finally, once they have fully grasped the significance of the underlying mathematical concepts and processes, they should be introduced to symbolic notation for recording their experiences (Symbols). *The abstraction process* (Skemp 1977), whereby learners come to represent and manipulate situations symbolically, is the most powerful feature of mathematics as a discipline. The ability to represent a physical act such as combining a set of three objects and a set of two objects with arbitrary symbols (e.g. 3 + 2) is fundamental to the abstraction process and is potentially the area most fraught with difficulty for the early years child. Mathematicians have taken centuries to devise and hone their procedures for performing calculations in the most efficient and elegant ways and it is often expected that young children will learn these abstracted techniques within a few years of schooling.

With its roots firmly planted in constructivist principles, emergent writing has become an accepted part of many teachers' early language activities. Less well known or adopted is '*emergent mathematics*' which has been proffered as a means of identifying and developing children's own mathematical awareness and understanding. Whitebread (1995) describes emergent mathematics as an approach that assumes children will develop an understanding of numbers by playing around with them, using them for their own purposes, talking about them with each other and adults, beginning to represent mathematical processes in ways that make sense to them and becoming more aware of their own and their teachers' mathematical thinking. Although this approach originally underpinned the National Numeracy Strategy (DfEE 1999), in some classrooms the purposes of the activities in the daily numeracy lesson advocated by the framework have lost their focus (Ofsted 2005).

Differing approaches to mathematics

Gravemeijer (1997) differentiates between teaching methods such as emergent mathematics which enable children to *construct* their own understanding and those which encourage children to *reconstruct* given mathematical knowledge as bottom–up and top–down respectively. Constructivist approaches are considered to be bottom–up in that they start from the child's understanding of the world and work outwards. By contrast to constructivism, behaviourist approaches to teaching and learning assume that knowledge and skills can be broken down into a series of incremental steps or stages and presented to the learner. Supporters of behaviourist approaches stress their value in enhancing observable, measurable behaviour, such as that which can be assessed through formal tests. Opponents note that the focus for behaviourist approaches is on the subject matter, often with assumptions that learners will be likely to follow a predetermined path and respond in predicted ways to the information that is presented. It could be argued that whereas constructivist inspired educational approaches focus on the learner, behaviourist based approaches centre on the learning material. And so, it should be expected that early years educators will be more amenable to constructivist approaches than those based on behaviourism.

Computer environments

From the point of view of the early years child and teacher the most valuable features of modern computer systems are the graphic user interface and the computer's ability to present information through a multimedia environment. In other words, today's computers are designed to communicate with the user with pictures, sounds, text and symbols, and the user can communicate with the computer by simply moving a mouse and clicking a button or two. The modern computer's ability to present the young learner with attractive animated visual images, text, icons, symbols, sound effects, music and natural speech should provide the child with a highly stimulating and effective learning environment. We have seen that one of the greatest difficulties for the development of children's mathematical understanding is the abstraction of first hand experience, through visual imagery, by the representation of situations with symbols. One might expect that the computer's ability to present information visually and symbolically could provide the ideal mathematics learning environment. It follows that one ought to find a plethora of high quality software for schools which is based on established constructivist principles. In reality, the majority of mathematics software used in schools (and the home) has its origins in the behaviourist model of learning with mathematical ideas being broken down into a series of incremental steps with children being guided towards a predetermined outcome. In England, school inspectors have reported that 'there is a disappointingly high use of programs providing drill and practice, which adds little to pupils' IT capability' (Ofsted 1995a: 13). The situation has changed little in ten years where inspectors report, 'Unimaginative software for number, spelling or tasks that are unrelated to pupils' needs or to work in the rest of the lesson contributes little' (Ofsted 2005: 19)

Both *'drill'* and *'practice'* were terms used by Skinner (1962) and his co-workers to describe aspects of programmed learning. The phrase 'drill and practice' was coined by early users of information technology to describe particular types of software which adopt a top–down approach (Suppes 1967). Mathematics programs which fit into this category offer children discrete activities to help them enhance their speed and accuracy in performing tasks such as numeral or shape recognition, recalling number facts such as multiplication products, addition bonds or provide practice exercises in performing calculations. Users are usually rewarded if successful (positive reinforcement) and sometimes reminded when they are unsuccessful. A useful benefit for the teacher is that some (a minority) programs log the children's progress and provide a report of each child's errors which could be used for the diagnosis of conceptual and/or procedural difficulties.

By comparison with the availability of mathematics software that has behaviourist roots, programs which can be used to support emergent or constructivist approaches to teaching and learning are relatively few in number. An analysis of the software offered to support early years mathematics teaching by a leading educational supplier revealed that of 88 titles listed in their catalogue and website, 48 (55%) provided practice activities for basic number skills, 11 programs (12.5%) were designed to introduce children to aspects of shape and space (e.g. shape naming and recognition) and most of the remainder (24%) covered specific topics such as time or sorting and classifying objects. Only five programs (6%) related mathematical activities to real contexts (e.g. shopping or running a hot dog stand) and two (2%) claimed to encourage children's logical thinking. Interestingly, only one piece of software in the numeracy and mathematics section was based on LOGO.

A constructionist computer environment

LOGO was devised by a team led by Seymour Papert and Wallace Feurzeig at the Massachusetts Institute of Technology in the 1960s. Papert, a student of Piaget, was convinced that the power of the microcomputer could be harnessed to support children's emergent mathematical thinking. At the heart of LOGO is turtle graphics. By programming a turtle to move with a series of instructions, Papert (1980) asserts that children's thinking becomes accessible to both the learner themselves and the teacher. Papert sees the turtle as an 'object-to-think-with ... supporting children as they build their own intellectual structures with materials drawn from the surrounding culture' (1980: 11, 32). With LOGO's origins firmly rooted in Piagetian theory, it provides the ideal computer-based constructivist learning environment, though Papert (1994) posits the notion of '*constructionism*' as the foundation for his work. According to Papert (1994), constructionism assumes that the most useful sort of knowledge is that which enables the child to get more knowledge. Thus, rather than focusing on improving their methods of instruction, to improve the quality of mathematics teaching, teachers should develop better ways of helping children learn how to learn – in much the same way as it is considered to be more useful to teach someone how to fish than it is to give them a fish when they are facing starvation.

Conflicting claims have been made as to the efficacy of LOGO in helping young children to develop mathematical understanding. Advocates of LOGO point to its value in bridging the gap between concrete experience and abstract representation (Anderson 1986); developing logical, analytical and lateral thinking skills (Blythe 1990); enhancing young children's facility to handle and explain numbers larger than those normally expected for a particular age group (Straker 1989); enabling children as young as 6 to develop generalised problem solving skills (Lawler 1997); markedly improving 6-year-old children's ability to reason in areas of spatial awareness and metacognition, as measured by cognitive tests (Clements and Gullo 1984); and providing a rich environment for the development of young children's early mathematical concepts of number and shape (Hughes and McLeod 1986).

By contrast, Pea and Kurland (1983) found no transfer of strategic thinking from LOGO to non-LOGO activities and Clements and Battista (1990) found that children who use LOGO can develop erroneous conceptions about angular measurement which are difficult for teachers to counter.

Using LOGO with young children

One of the greatest difficulties with making use of LOGO in the classroom is the considerable investment in time which is required both on the part of the teacher and the children. Some approaches attempt to overcome this drawback by providing children with a series of structured tasks (Howe et al. 1984) designed to teach children basic knowledge of LOGO programming techniques through 'guided discovery learning' (Finlayson

1983: 12). Clearly, top–down approaches such as these conflict with the constructivist (or constructionist) principles on which LOGO is founded. However, they provide support for teachers who are not familiar or confident with using LOGO in the classroom. This highlights another major problem associated with the use of content-free software such as LOGO; the more open-ended the software, the greater the requirement for preparation, input and support on the part of the teacher. Bottom–up approaches to teaching with LOGO rely on the teacher having knowledge of and sympathy for constructivist principles and having the practical skills and confidence to put these into effect. More importantly, they require sustained access to the computer by the children with frequent opportunities for teacher intervention which is not realistic in an early years classroom with only one computer (Simon et al. 1987; Ainley and Pratt 1995).

Preparatory activities for LOGO turtle graphics

Papert and his co-workers used a computer controlled floor robot to precede or accompany initial screen-based work in guiding the turtle – thus strengthening in the children's minds the links between enactive experience, pictorial representation and the abstract symbolic commands controlling the movements of the turtle. As indicated by Carol Fine and Mary Lou Thornbury in Chapter 2, these days, programmable robots or turtles are commonly found in primary schools and can provide valuable preparatory experience for screen-based LOGO turtle graphics. By pressing keys on the back of the turtle, the children can enter a series of instructions to guide the turtle around, for example, a simple maze. They can be used to reinforce children's understanding of numbers by programming the turtle to move forwards and backwards along a number line (Page 2000) or can introduce the children to angular measurement through the requirement to specify the amount of turn required (Blythe 1990). Most programmable turtles can be configured to re-scale the size of the units used by the turtle. For example, the turtle can be programmed to turn one degree or one quarter of a complete turn when the child enters 'LEFT 1'. Some computer programs provide a link between this type of first-hand experience with programmable toys and LOGO turtle graphics software which initially shows an intimidating, featureless, blank screen. Some software provides opportunities for children to sequence a series of actions, such as *Playground* (Topologika) in which the children 'program' Freddy Teddy to use various pieces of playground equipment. Another approach is to make the LOGO environment more attractive by presenting a 'microworld' for the children to explore. In some microworlds, the turtle becomes a character who must be guided through adventure-type scenarios or a series of mazes (e.g. *Roamer World*, Valiant; *Terry the Turtle*, Kudlian Soft). *LOGO MicroWorlds* (LCSI) combines a set of simple multi-media graphics, sound and animation tools with LOGO programming commands to enable children and/or teachers to create their own microworlds (see also Chapter 6: Games and Simulations, p. 87).

Data handling and constructivist teaching approaches

Another opportunity for open-ended activities which can be used to support a constructivist approach to teaching and learning is provided by data handling software. The most basic of these are graphing packages, which enable the child to enter a set of data and, with minimal effort, select and display a range of graphs. Thus, the computer is used as a tool to facilitate the children's manipulation and presentation of meaningful data. If data handling software is used in the most effective way, emphasis is thrown more on the posing and answering of children's own questions through gathering data and interpreting results (Bennett 1997). Often, without the computer too much emphasis is placed on drawing and colouring graphs and important opportunities to make effective use of data to further children's understanding of numbers in real contexts are lost (Jared and Thwaites 1995; Ofsted, 1995b).

In the nursery and early years situation, the database work will focus on sorting and classifying with real objects, since this is of prime importance at this stage. Such early practical work will lead on later to the use of very simple programs using sorting and classification as their basis. For example, the children can be physically sorted into height order or into sets according to hair colour. Objects can similarly be sorted to enable the children to make the connection between the objects and the reality they represent. Practical activities with the real objects and their pictorial representations are an essential precursor to any data handling activity with computers, to ensure that the children have clear mental models of the processes which the database is replicating, when it sorts, selects or graphs.

At the most elementary level, simple counting or graphing programs can be used to record and represent first hand experiences, such as sorting fruit into categories and finding out which is the most common. Many programs enable the teacher or a child to present the information as a pictogram and then switch to a block graph or a bar chart with the click of a mouse button. This seemingly unremarkable feature holds immense potential for developing children's understanding of the relationship between the bar chart and what it represents. It also can lay the foundations for enabling children to relate abstract numerals to sets of objects. Imagine the children sorting cuddly toys into different sets of animals. They have a collection of teddy bears, rabbits, mice and a seal. They rearrange the animals into groups on the carpet and see that there are more teddy bears than any other animal. They 'count' the teddy bears by clicking a button on the computer screen, one click for each bear in the pile. As they click a similar group appears on the screen. The group on the screen shows a stack of teddy bears similar to their stack. The children therefore make the connection between the group on the screen and the bears on the carpet – they have made the link between first hand experience and the pictures which represent this experience. They see that the bears' group on the screen is bigger than the groups representing the other animals. The teacher clicks a button and the group of teddy bears changes instantaneously into a column of blocks. Another click and the blocks are numbered from one to five. Another click and the blocks change into a continuous column with an adjacent axis. All the time the teacher is asking the children to explain what they are seeing, what the columns and the numbers represent. The computer has enabled the children to see that the numeral 5 represents the number of teddy bears arranged on the carpet.

The graphs are printed out and displayed on the wall so the children can refer to them and recall the experiences which they represent. Hence, the ability of the computer to represent images with shapes and symbols has been used to help children build mental models of the situation.

Structuring activities to systematically support the development of children's thinking is termed '*scaffolding*' by constructivists (Bruner 1978: 19). In the same way that scaffolding is used on a building site to assist with the construction of a building, it is argued that teachers should scaffold activities for children, enabling them to build their own understanding – understanding which remains stable when the 'scaffolding' is removed. Data handling lends itself to scaffolding but only if the 'data' being handled are real and familiar to the children, so the increasingly abstract representations then remain meaningful.

A drawback of some databases is that they can inspire a notion of a black box mystery. The children carry out a series of tasks that result in an outcome which is of little relevance to them and hence carries minimal meaning. As discussed by Rosemary Feasey and Margaret Still in Chapter 5, purposeful data handling is enquiry led. It starts with a question, preferably a question which is meaningful for the children and, better still one which they are particularly interested in answering. For example, a group of Year 1 children was interested in finding out whether different types of fruit floated or sank when put in water. Initially, they predicted which would float and which would sink. They then tested their predictions and were surprised to discover some of their predictions were inaccurate. When the teacher said that she was also surprised by the result the children wondered whether adults would be any better at predicting the results than they had been. How could they find out? They needed to ask a sample of adults which types of fruit they thought would float and which would sink. The children were very excited by the prospect of asking adults a question to which they knew the answer and, as it turned out, many adults did not. Once they had accumulated the answers and put the information into the database they were able to ask and answer more questions. Were women better at predicting which types of fruit floated than men? Did the people who predicted that bananas would sink also believe that kiwi fruits would sink? – and so on.

The advantage of the database over pencil and paper is the speed and accuracy with which the data can be manipulated and presented. In the above example, all the men who were questioned could be selected and their predictions graphed – then all the women could be selected and their predictions graphed. Similarly, all those who predicted that bananas would float could be selected and a graph produced showing these people's other predictions. To be able to make use of databases in this way teachers need to be very familiar with how databases work and the tools that they offer (i.e. sorting, selecting, searching, graphing) – and how to structure activities carefully to ensure the children can make connections between what is on the screen and the reality that is being represented.

The role of the teacher

As with LOGO, the successful use of data handling software in the early years classroom is reliant on the teacher being able to ensure the tasks relate to children's existing knowledge. The role of the teacher is of critical importance in supporting a constructivist approach to learning. The teacher must 'scaffold' experiences to support children's knowledge building (Bruner 1978: 19), not only through the provision of appropriate activities but also by the use of carefully considered questioning and explanation. The first Impact Report (Watson 1993), a government sponsored study of the impact of ICT on children's achievements in schools, found that the most significant factor affecting children's effective use of the computer was the role of the teacher. This was not only in terms of organizing and managing the resources but, 'teaching styles, philosophy as to the nature of the subject, and pedagogical practice and their links with the effective use of IT were found to be important contributors [to the outcomes of pupils' learning]' (Watson 1993: 1). The main implication of the Impact Project's findings is that the way the computer is used with children is just as important as the software. This view is reinforced by Squires and McDougall (1994) who enter into a comprehensive discourse on the categorization and use of educational software. Their conclusions are that simplistic checklists of software types with decontextualised evaluations of their effectiveness can be misleading. They posit an evaluative paradigm, which takes account of the ways in which a program is used in the classroom as a more effective, reliable and worthwhile approach. Their paradigm centres on consideration of the interactions between the learner, the teacher and the designer of the software (Bennett 1997). In essence, Squires and McDougall suggest that the evaluation of software should focus on the locus of control. Software is likely to be more educationally effective if it places control more in the hands of the learner than of the teacher or designer (of the program). They suggest, however, the interaction of the teacher and the software with the child, will have a significant effect on the educational value of a learning experience at the computer. As we have seen, although LOGO was designed to be used in a way which put the learner firmly in control, the use of structured LOGO activities can shift the locus of control towards the teacher (i.e. as the provider of the structured tasks). While open-ended software such as LOGO and databases can be used in a range of different ways, from highly structured teacher devised tasks to learner led activities, more prescriptive, computer centred programs offer far less flexibility in their application. Thus, a drill and practice program designed to present children with a series of computer generated questions will offer little scope for placing control in the hands of the learner or the teacher. The role of the teacher is therefore of critical importance; not only in selecting software but also in devising, setting and supporting computer based learning activities. In a small scale study, McCraw and Meyer (1995: 4) noted 'that the use of the computer most often paralleled the individual teacher's instructional style. When classroom teachers used direct instruction rather than discovery learning, they most likely used the computer in the same way'. This would imply that early years teachers' over-reliance on drill and practice software indicates that they tend to adopt behaviourist inspired approaches to the teaching of mathematics. This seems to contradict the child centred principles on which early years education has been founded.

What software is used in schools at present?

To evaluate the way teachers were making use of ICT in their numeracy and mathematics teaching, the author conducted a small scale survey of local schools. The teachers in 28 schools across three local authorities were surveyed by questionnaire, representing a cross section of school types, from a small rural primary with three teachers to a large urban school with 14 teachers. Ninety teachers responded to the survey with 59 (66%) providing additional written comments in response to open questions asking for their opinions on the value and practicalities of using ICT in their teaching. Three teachers were informally interviewed to triangulate the findings. Eight per cent of early years teachers (n = 41) in the survey confessed to making no use of information and communications technology to support, enhance or extend their teaching of mathematics or numeracy. However, not all teachers responded to the survey and it might be that among those who did not respond there was a high proportion of non-ICT users. There is a statutory requirement for teachers to use ICT in all subject areas (apart from PE) and this might have deterred some respondents from submitting null returns even though the questionnaires were completed anonymously.

Teachers were asked to identify the programs and applications they used most frequently to support their teaching of numeracy and mathematics. They were also invited to describe how the programs were used.

The age distribution in the classes surveyed ranged from mixed age classes, including vertically grouped classes covering the whole early years age group to a school in which there were 75 children in a single year group distributed among three classes. The numbers of children in the classes ranged from 11 (in a special needs unit) to 36. (See Figure 4.1.)

The type of software used by the teachers fell mostly into the drill and practice category. Fourteen teachers indicated use of data handling software, one on a daily basis. Mostly this type of application was used termly, or 'as required'. Only one teacher used LOGO, though four teachers mentioned the use of the Roamer programmable turtle (classed as 'other'). (See Figure 4.2.)

Practice, reinforcement, consolidation, counting and number recognition were the activities mentioned most and carried out most frequently. In the main these activities were performed daily, or 'on most days' or weekly. Data handling and graph making were the next most popular activities, but these activities tended to happen 'as appropriate', termly or once a year, whenever the relevant topic was being taught. (See Figure 4.3.)

It would appear that this small scale survey reinforces the findings of Ofsted (1995a; 2005) that the most frequent use of computer technology

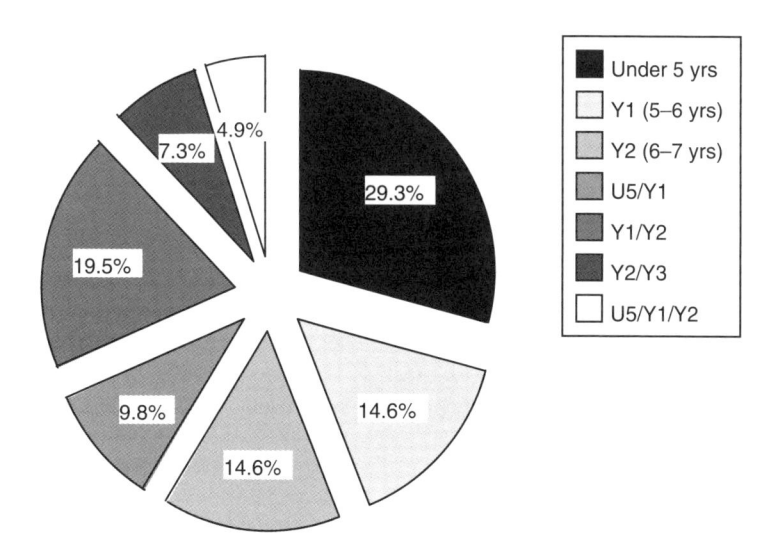

Figure 4.1 Age distribution in the classes taught (n = 41)

ICT IN THE EARLY YEARS

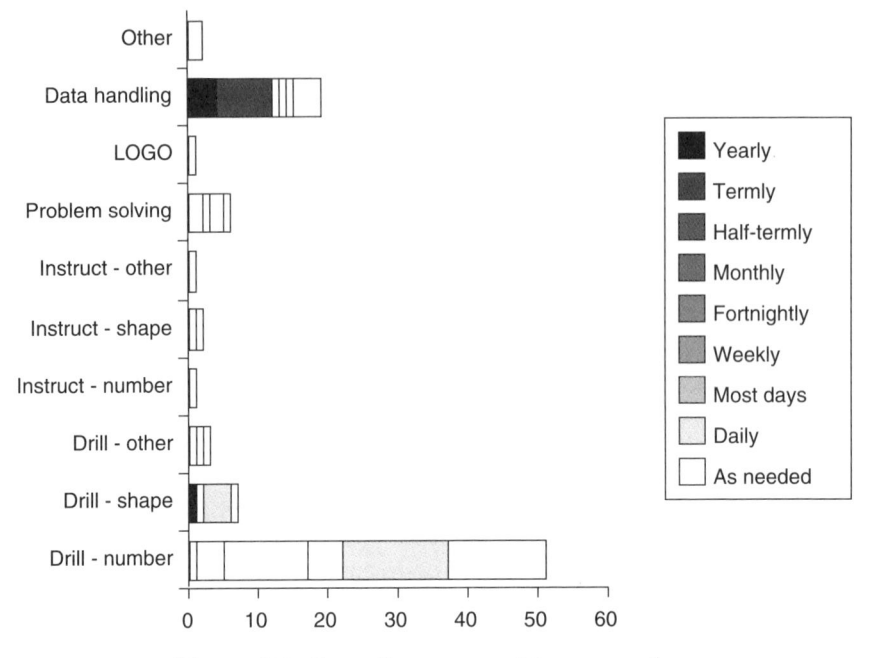

Figure 4.2 Type of program and frequency of use

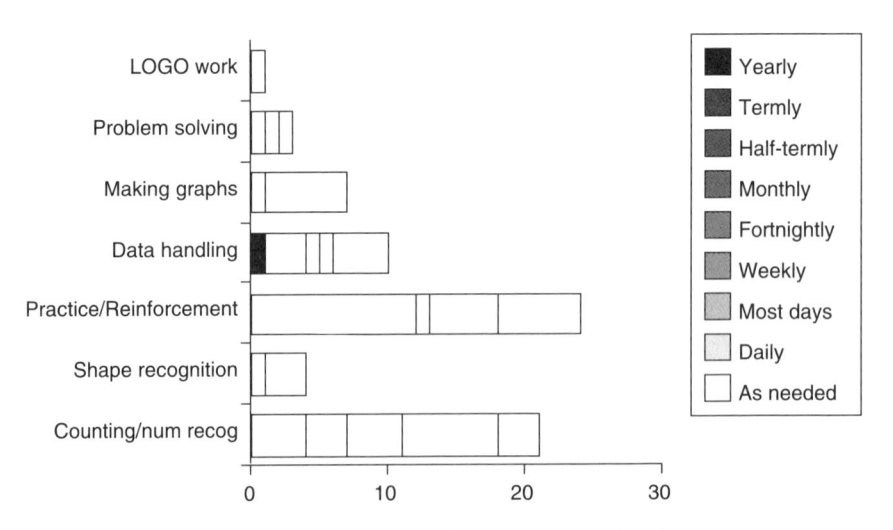

Figure 4.3 Frequency of computer based activity

for supporting numeracy work in the early years classroom is for drill and practice. But should this be surprising or worrying? Does it necessarily follow that a preponderance of this type of computer use implies ineffective, ineffectual or insufficient use of the computer for supporting the teaching and learning of mathematics? Does this necessarily reflect the teaching styles for mathematics that early years teachers adopt, as suggested by McCraw and Meyer (1995)?

The written comments from the teachers provide some insights. Many teachers (39%) indicated that they were enthusiastic about using the computer by describing the positive benefits for motivation and learning: 'It is very good for encouraging children as they are all very enthusiastic and regard it as fun and games rather than learning' (Reception teacher). And, 'Computers add another dimension to classroom teaching – Children enjoy the interaction and realise that it can mean a speedy completion of some chores' (Reception/Year 1 teacher).

Some teachers commented that this was dependent on the quality of the software and the relevance of the activities. For example: 'ICT is definitely worth the effort. The children enjoy using the programs and gain a lot from them. When they work in pairs they often generate good discussions and ideas. They particularly enjoy the colourful graphics and any sounds the software may include' (Reception class teacher).

However, the most frequent comment (57%) pointed to the restrictions imposed by the lack of adult support. For example, 'Although it is worth the effort, it can be difficult to manage, especially without classroom support. The teacher usually has to help children with their work, which limits the time you can spend with children at the computer' (Reception class teacher). A Year 2 teacher said, 'I feel it [ICT] is a great aid but it would work more effectively if there were more computers in school and more staff to work solely on the computer with individuals. The class teacher doesn't always have time to spend with pupils as [he or she] is teaching the rest of the class and supporting them'. And,

> The use of ICT with reception [children] depends on extra adult help. Children thoroughly enjoy the programs especially the newer CD-ROM titles – but can only use these with an adult – other than the class teacher. The class teacher cannot sit with individual children or be constantly interrupted when programs go wrong. It is clearly not a sensible use of the class teacher's time.
>
> (Reception class teacher)

It would seem that despite a predominance of computer controlled software (e.g. drill and practice), teachers find they do not have sufficient time to work with the children at the computer. Others felt hamstrung by the additional demands placed on them in trying to manage the technology: 'Often difficult in a reception class with no classroom support. It is a very good learning tool and a good source of motivation but often very stressful for the teacher to administer!' (Reception class teacher). And, 'If you are well resourced and have appropriate help/assistance all is fine. *But*, more often than not, things go wrong (printers don't work, computers get viruses) and the whole thing seems more trouble than it's worth' (Year 2 teacher, original emphasis).

It would appear that, with one computer in the classroom, it is easier to use drill and practice programs than to work with small groups and computerised toys, LOGO activities or data handling activities. Some early years schools or departments have opted to replace or augment their classroom computers with a computer suite. While this does overcome some of the management difficulties and children's contact time is increased, there is still a tendency to use drill and practice software for reinforcement as indicated by the four teachers in the survey who had regular access to a computer room. What is really needed is good quality software which meets teachers' management and curricular needs, while presenting activities which are based on sound constructivist educational practices.

What software should we be looking for?

Heppell (1994: 154) observes that 'over a millennium or so we have developed a variety of fairly clear ideas about some of the components of successful learning but there is little evidence these have been absorbed by other than a few commercial multimedia designers'. He goes on to suggest that most software designers assume the deficiency model of children's learning and he argues that they should 'recognise the emergent capability of learners and respond to the climate of expectation that those learners bring to their computer screens' (p. 158). His response was an attempt to address software design features specified by teachers, parents and children by devising a program for multiplication. Heppell would seem to be suggesting that computer controlled software is what teachers, parents and children want. By contrast, Hennesey et al. (1988, 1991) developed a piece of mathematics software based on constructivist learning principles. Their 'intelligent computer tutor for informal arithmetic' (Hennesey et al. 1991: 295) presented an imaginary context (*Shopping on Mars*) in which children were invited to solve problems and model their individualistic calculation strategies on the screen through a 'Graphics Arithmetic Description Language (GADL)'. Not only were children working within a multimedia context which was of interest to them, but they were also encouraged and supported in making explicit their idiosyncratic calculation strategies – precisely what the Numeracy Strategy aims to promote. Unfortunately, *Shopping on Mars* was never made available commercially.

Multimedia computer systems offer immense potential for early years mathematics education by bridging the gap between concrete experience and abstract representation. The majority of mathematics software currently available for the early years classroom is based on a deficit model of children's knowledge and understanding and would appear to require considerable effort in terms of planning, management and intervention by the teacher. Perhaps the time has come for serious funding to be put into the development of software based on sound educational principles which takes account of the organizational implications of the early years classroom. After all, what use is an expensive computer if the software does not address the needs of the learner, the teacher or the mathematics curriculum?

References

Ainley, J. and Pratt, D.C. (1995) Planning for portability: Integrating mathematics and technology in the primary curriculum, in L. Burton and B. Jaworski (eds) *Technology and Mathematics Teaching: A Bridge Between Teaching and Learning*. Bromley: Chartwell Bratt.

Anderson, B. (1986) *Learning with LOGO: Some Classroom Experiences*. Loughborough: Microelectronics Education Programme.

Bennett, R. (1997) *Teaching IT*. Oxford: Nash Pollock.

Blythe, K. (1990) *Children Learning with LOGO*. Coventry: National Council for Educational Technology.

Bruner, J. (1978) The role of dialogue in language acquisition, in A. Sinclair, R. Jarvella and W.J.M. Levelt (eds) *The Children's Conception of Language*. New York: Springer-Verlag.

Clements, D.H. and Battista, M.T. (1990) The effects of Logo on children's conceptualisations of angle and polygons, *Journal for Research in Mathematics Education*, 21: 356–71.

Clements, D.H. and Gullo, D.F. (1984) Effects of computer programming on young children's cognition, *Journal of Educational Psychology*, 76: 1051–8.

DfEE (1999) *The National Numeracy Strategy: Framework for Teaching Mathematics from Reception to Year 6*. London: Department for Education and Employment.

Finlayson, H. (1983) Simple LOGO in Primary Schools: A structured or unstructured approach? *Micro-Scope LOGO Special*. Birmingham: MAPE & BLUG, Newman College.

Froebel, F. ([1887] 1992) in J. Moore, Early years experience in Denmark and England: The place of information technology, *Early Years*, 12(2): 36–40.

Gelman R. and Gallistel, C.R. (1978) *The Child's Understanding of Number*. Cambridge, MA: Harvard University Press.

Gravemeijer, K. (1997) Mediating between concrete and abstract, in T. Nanes and P. Bryant, (eds) *Learning and Teaching Mathematics: An International Perspective*. Hove: Psychology Press.

Hennessy, S., Evertsz, R., Ellis, D. et al. (1988) *Design Specification for 'Shopping on Mars': A Computer-based Educational Activity*. CITE technical report no. 29, The Open University.

Hennesey, S., O'Shea, T., Evertsz, R. and Floyd, A. (1991) An intelligent tutoring system approach to teaching primary mathematics, in O. Boyd-Barrett and E. Scanlon (eds) *Computers and Learning*. Wokingham: Addison Wesley.

Heppell, S. (1994) Multimedia and learning: Normal children, normal lives and real change, in J. Underwood (ed.) *Computer Based Learning: Potential into Practice*. London: David Fulton.

Howe, J.A.M., Ross, P.M., Johnson, K.R. and Inglis, R. (1984) Model building, mathematics and LOGO, in M. Yazdani (ed.) *New Horizons in Educational Computing*. Chichester: Ellis Horwood.

Hughes, M. (1986) *Children and Number: Difficulties in Learning Mathematics*. Oxford: Blackwell.

Hughes, M. and McLeod, H. (1986) Using LOGO with very young children, in R.W. Lawler, B. Du Boulay and H. McLeod (eds) *Cognition and Computers: Studies in Learning*. Chichester: Ellis Horwood.

Jared, E. and Thwaites, A. (1995) What is your favourite colour? in J. Anghileri (ed.) *Children's Mathematical Thinking the Primary's Learning*. London: Cassell.

Lawler, R. W. (1997) *Learning with Computers*. Exeter: Intellect Books.

Liebeck, P. (1984) *How Children Learn Mathematics: A Guide for Parents and Teachers*. Harmondsworth: Penguin.

McCraw, P.A. and Meyer, J.E. (1995) *Technology and Young Children: What Teachers Need to Know*. Available at http://www.coe.uh.edu/insite/elec_pub/html1995/0816.htm (accessed 16 March 2000).

Ofsted (1995a) *Information Technology: A Review of Inspection Findings 1993/4*. London: HMSO.

Ofsted (1995b) *Mathematics: A Review of Inspection Findings 1993/4*. London: HMSO.

Ofsted (1998) *The National Numeracy Project: An HMI Evaluation*. London: Office for Standards in Education.

Ofsted (2005) *The National Literacy and Numeracy Strategies and the Primary Curriculum*. London: Office for Standards in Education.

Page, V. (2000) *Reception class children, a Roamer Turtle and a number line: Introducing number concepts with a programmable toy*. Unpublished MEd Project, University College Chester.

Papert, S. (1980) *Mindstorms: Children, Computers and Powerful Ideas*. Hemel Hempstead: Harvester Wheatsheaf.

Papert, S. (1994) *The Children's Machine: Rethinking School in the Age of the Computer*. Hemel Hempstead: Harvester Wheatsheaf.

Pea, R.D. and Kurland, D.M. (1983) *LOGO Programming and the Development of Planning Skills: Technical Report No. 16*. New York: Center for Children and Technology, Bank St College.

Simon, T., McShane, J. and Radley, S. (1987) Learning with microcomputers: Training primary school children on a problem-solving program, *Applied Cognitive Psychology*, 1: 35–44.

Skemp, R.R. (1971) *The Psychology of Learning Mathematics*. Harmondsworth: Penguin.

Skemp, R.R. (1977) *The Psychology of Learning Mathematics*. Harmondsworth: Penguin.

Skinner, B.F. (1962) Squirrel in the yard: certain sciurine experiences, *Harvard Alumni Bulletin*, 64: 642–5.

Skinner, B.F. (1968) *The Technology of Teaching*. London: Appleton Century Crofts.

Squires, D. and McDougall, A. (1994) *Choosing and Using Educational Software: A Teachers' Guide*. London: Falmer.

Straker, A. (1989) *Children Using Computers*. Oxford: Blackwell Education.

Suppes, P. (1967) The teacher and computer-assisted instruction, *NEA Journal*, (February) 67.

Watson, D. (1993) *The Impact Summary: An Evaluation of the Impact of Information Technology on Children's Achievements in Primary and Secondary Schools*. London: Department for Education and King's College, London.

Whitebread, D. (1995) Emergent Mathematics or How to Help Young Children become Confident Mathematicians, in J. Anghileri (ed.) *Children's Thinking in Primary Mathematics: Perspectives on Children's Learning*. London: Cassell.

5
SCIENCE AND ICT

Rosemary Feasey and Margaret Still

Introduction

In this chapter key issues relating to the relationship between information and communications technology (ICT) and science are discussed. The aims of this chapter are three fold: the first is to suggest how ICT supports learning in science; the second aim is to explore how using ICT in science can assist the development of the whole child, in particular positive learning dispositions; and the third aim is to illustrate these points and issues through a number of ICT applications in early years science. No attempt is made to cover every application of ICT in science. Instead a number of areas have been selected to raise the profile of their potential and challenge some current practices.

This chapter is predicated on the viewpoint that young children have the potential to become ICT literate in science at a very early age and that children should be given access to a wide range of applications in science from the moment they enter formal schooling. It takes an approach similar to that of Carr (2001: 11) who views learning in science as a 'credit model'. As Siraj-Blatchford and Siraj-Blatchford (1995: 2) point out: 'Even the youngest children bring with them into school understandings, skills, knowledge and attitudes, and it is the teacher's role to help them

SCIENCE AND ICT

develop and build upon these'. Feasey and Gallear (2001: 5) take this a step further and contextualise the point in relation to ICT in science when they suggest that:

> Children at the beginning of the 21st century live in a world where they have access to the Internet, digital clocks, digital bathroom scales, video machines and computers which allow children to scan, take and store photographs and desktop publish.
>
> Today's children expect to have a mobile phone to communicate with friends and family, their watches light up and make strange noises and their leisure time is often spent playing complex computer games. Children's lives are surrounded by the products of the information and communication age; children not only live in a technological age, they are the technological age.

Most young children enter formal schooling with some understanding of ICT and some personal experience and skills. Science must build on this as part of the development of sound foundations to ensure that by the end of the primary years they are competent, confident, motivated and critical users of ICT in this area of the curriculum.

Given that children are the 'technological age' teachers must be prepared to offer children access to a range of ICT regardless of the teacher's own personal capability. The teacher needs to reconsider his or her role and, where necessary, shift from being the 'expert' to the 'learner' alongside the child. Later in this chapter this issue will be raised again in relation to the introduction of the Intel Play Computer Microscope into all primary schools in England.

The key focus regarding using ICT to support teaching and learning in science is not, 'Can I, the teacher, manage to use the equipment?' but rather on the 'fitness for purpose' of ICT in a given situation. As Feasey and Gallear (2001: 5) state, the most important question we must ask ourselves as teachers, is 'How will this enhance the science teaching and learning for these children?'

While the focus of this chapter is the relationship between science and ICT, early years education is about the whole child and not about subjects taken in isolation. It is therefore important to remember that using ICT in science is not just about a child learning, for example, to use a digital camera, a computer or sensors, but also it is a means for contributing to the wider development of each individual child and indeed to the broader aims of science education. De Boo (2000: 6) points out that:

> The ultimate aim of education is to produce well-informed, scientifically literate citizens who can find things out for themselves, look critically at media or other information and make long-term decisions about their world, for themselves and the environment. The future is in their hands

– the better we can educate our young children, the better that future will be.

Learning dispositions

To lay the foundations of the scientifically literate individual and to help develop children's understanding of scientific concepts and skills, children need to have a 'positive learning disposition' towards science and the use of ICT.

Early years educators are familiar with the idea of learning dispositions. Carr (2001: 21) explains that a positive learning disposition is:

> Being ready, willing and able to participate in various ways . . . in which the teacher takes the child to the next step in a task, gives some assistance, and then gradually withdraws the assistances so that the child can perform the skill all by her- or himself – assumes, as Goodnow (1990) commented, a picture not only of 'willing' teachers on the one hand but of 'eager' learners on the other.

Carr quotes Lilian Katz (1988: 30) who offers this interpretation of learning dispositions: 'Dispositions are a very different type of learning from skills and knowledge. They can be thought of as habits of mind, tendencies to respond to situations in certain ways'. Carr quotes Claxton (1990: 164) who comments that: 'it can be strongly argued that schools' major responsibility must be to help young people become ready, willing and able to cope with change successfully: that is, to be powerful and effective learners'.

In early years science this is exactly what the teacher is attempting to do, to encourage positive dispositions towards learning in science by engaging children in a range of activities to develop their ability to think and work scientifically. In order for this to be successful the teacher needs to offer children an environment that is sympathetic to developing positive dispositions. In terms of science, this includes providing interesting and stimulating experiences within a planned framework to ensure success for individuals. In science, positive learning dispositions include:

- Taking an interest
- Being involved
- Persisting with difficulty or uncertainty
- Communicating with others
- Taking responsibility.

Successful science relies on developing positive learning dispositions alongside sound teaching and learning approaches. As De Boo (2000: 12) indicates:

Adult intervention throughout is a vital ingredient. Teachers, classroom assistants, nursery nurses and parents all act as role models for the developing child. Adults who are uninterested or less enthusiastic about the world around them, who show no curiosity or interest in things, will send negative messages about science. Conversely, adults who are enthusiastic, questioning, value new experiences and have an obvious love for learning will provide positive role models for children.

An important role of ICT in science is to support the development of positive dispositions in this area of the early years curriculum. Hence the need for those adults involved in supporting early years science to be creative, enthusiastic and open minded in the teaching and learning approaches they develop in early years settings. The positive use of ICT to support science learning is therefore crucial to the development of not only scientific concepts and skills but also to the whole child:

> It is absolutely essential that we pay particular attention to children's dispositions and feelings if they are to be successful in acquiring knowledge and skills. If we want children to gain a sound knowledge and understanding of science then we must encourage a positive learning disposition towards the subject. Underachievement, apathy, or even resistance in adolescence usually begins with some degree of discouragement in the early years.
>
> (De Boo 2000: 57)

In all of this rhetoric it is the individual child who helps to put things into perspective, reminding us that all children are individuals, with different starting points. Some children have well-developed learning dispositions towards science and ICT, sometimes coming to school confident and competent because of experiences in the home. Others require considerable encouragement to bring them out of their uncertainty and reticence because of their lack of exposure prior to formal schooling to science and ICT. Feasey in De Boo (2000) offers this salutary experience to underpin the need to accept and work with individuals' starting points.

> Two nursery-age children were working at a computer on a simple program for sorting animals. One child was actively involved, the other stood behind watching.
>
> Adult: You are very busy, you look as though you are an expert at sorting the animals, are you?
> Child 1: Yes, I can put the animals in different squares.
> Adult: (To Child 2) Are you an expert as well?
> Child 2: My name is Philip.
>
> (De Boo 2000: 36)

The role of ICT in science

Acknowledging that science and ICT have an important part to play in different aspects of the individual child's development, let us consider specifically the issue of how ICT can contribute to early years science.

Frost (1995: 9) offers an important point in relation to the use of ICT in science:

> When teachers started using the technology in class, other advantages became apparent. When their pupils became fluent in using sensors, the computer offered a new insight into science: they gained something that helped them to understand and encouraged them to explore. When the children used databases and spreadsheets they didn't just draw graphs, they could go onto interpret them. And when they worked together with a word processor, they started talking with zeal, not the usual gossip, but about science.

Frost continues and suggests that ICT offers very special tools, which he calls 'the tools of the mind'. This is an apt phrase because where ICT applications in science are used appropriately they should support the teacher in challenging children to 'engage brain', by drawing upon personal scientific knowledge and understanding as well as everyday experiences and skills.

When children use any ICT application in science, and 'engage brain', the adult should be encouraging children to participate in making a range of decisions such as what, when and how to use it.

The extent to which children will be able to work independently will depend upon the depth of their experience, personal confidence and disposition to using ICT in science. With very young children there will be a partnership with those adults working with individuals and groups. The role of the adult in the partnership is to scaffold and enable children to use their increasing competence to become more and more independent, in both the ICT and the science. It would be naïve to assume that this transition to becoming expert occurs solely within early years, indeed for most children, the transition will not be completed until they enter secondary schooling and maybe not until later in life.

Frost's 'tools of the mind' encompasses many different aspects of working in science. One of the most important advantages of ICT is the access to data that some applications offer, allowing children to collect data automatically and immediately show the results. With very young children this is one of the most important advantages of ICT in science. Children can have access to immediate readouts and the computer can create a graph based on the data. The teacher can then challenge children to think about the data and to talk about the patterns, trends, oddities and draw conclusions.

As part of their scientific investigations, children gather information by observing and describing objects, animals and plants. They make collections, ask questions, talk about and describe the objects in front of them. They sort their collections into groups under simple criteria, as they look for and identify similarities and differences. They begin to classify scientifically but at the same time they are developing vital information handling skills, a prerequisite to much work within ICT. Sorting objects is a valuable, concrete experience for young children and, as an extension, these children can use simple computer programs that are designed to group pictures of objects by dragging them around the screen using the mouse. As they sort and group objects, children are beginning to develop skills of classification and the use of keywords. Sorting activities can be extended to producing a binary or classification tree. Children learn to pose questions that require a yes or no answer as they identify and understand similarities and differences. This activity is a process of questioning that encourages children to ask scientific questions using correct scientific vocabulary.

Effective questioning

A crucial part of 'tools of the mind' is developing children as effective questioners. Careful use of ICT in science can support this, and the role of the adult is to model effective questions and gradually share the responsibility with the children. For example:

- What shall we use?
- How will we use it?
- What can we see on the screen?
- What do you think it is?
- What does the graph say?
- What is the story of the graph?
- What do we want to know?
- How could the computer help us to find out what we know?

To achieve this children need a supportive environment that encourages questioning and supports approaches to finding an answer. Children need a framework and the teacher needs to model how to ask questions and answer them.

Communication in science

Another important area where ICT provides an excellent partnership with science is in the area of children communicating. ICT offers young children a range of alternatives from using the word processor, either personally or with the help of a scribe, to creating graphs, use paint tools and taking digital pictures. Access to this range can free some children from the shackles of having to write for themselves allowing them to indicate what they know through creating photographic records, tables, graphs, adding labels or matching pictures. The most important issue is not that children write about science but that they are able to communicate their ideas in different ways to a range of audiences.

Collaboration and co-operation

Science is often portrayed as being a solitary occupation carried out by manic looking individuals with few social skills. The opposite is of course true; science is a social activity, requiring a range of people with differing expertise to work together. Science also relies on the wider community to challenge and validate ideas as well as to share new information. Science in the classroom attempts to emulate this, challenging children to work co-operatively together on an activity or a problem that they need to solve. In the classroom we encourage children to talk, share ideas, think about consequences and consider alternatives, and to do so in a way that does not diminish contributions from different children, but instead values them.

Practical science activities should require children to share resources and also to support each other through peer tutoring, where one child is able to help another.

Instant feedback

ICT in science frequently offers children instant feedback, through sensors or a computer microscope. On one occasion I watched a group of young children using a program that asked them some simple questions related to a science topic. It challenged them to sort objects and generally helped them to revisit and revise some basic subject knowledge. The whole class clamoured to use it, they loved showing what they knew and were delighted when the cartoon character applauded them or the computer made a congratulatory sound. On completion they wanted to start all over again and were always eager to let the teacher know their score. What did they learn? Well they learned that they knew something, that they could succeed, that revising ideas and facts was fun and they were motivated to engage with the subject. Even those less certain who sat back and watched classmates were drawn into offering ideas when they felt confident to do so and were pleased for their friends when their answers were correct. They were, in a small and subtle way, developing positive learning dispositions in science.

In a different but similar way the digital camera, computer microscope

SCIENCE AND ICT

and sensors offer children immediate feedback; sometimes, as in the case of the computer microscope, this feedback is unexpected. A group of children looked at parts of their body using a computer microscope and were amazed to see the detail of their eye, hairs in their nose and the pattern of their skin.

Instant feedback of this kind also leads to the development of 'awe and wonder', contributing to the 'wow!' factor of science.

Classroom applications

In this section the focus is placed on three particular applications of ICT in science: the digital camera, computer sensors and the Intel Computer Microscope. These were chosen because of their excellent potential for:

- supporting the development of scientific concepts and skills;
- developing ICT skills;
- encouraging collaboration and communication;
- supporting the development of positive learning dispositions towards science and ICT.

One other important reason for choosing these three applications is that in many early years settings they are underused and their potential underestimated. Some ICT applications in science have, over the years, inadvertently become the province of the upper primary range and used less frequently in early years.

Language

Underpinning use of ICT applications in science is the need for the children to be exposed to three language genres, that of science and ICT as well as everyday language. Both science and ICT use specific language and successful communication in each requires children to become familiar with and use both. Take for example the use of temperature sensors:

Table 5.1 The language of science, ICT and everyday: the example of temperature sensors

Science	*ICT*	*Everyday*
Temperature	Sensor	Up
Thermometer	Program	Down
Degrees	Probe	Hot
Hot	Display	Cold
Cold		Touch
change		Feel

Children will need to be taught the language, as Feasey in De Boo (2000: 28) suggests, 'As adults we take for granted the language we use on a daily basis ... we are sometimes in danger of forgetting how challenging it can be for children to express themselves, especially in relation to ideas and experiences that are new to them'. Feasey in De Boo (2000) quotes Deforges (1989:43) who suggests that 'one of the major tasks of early years childhood education is to mange the transition to concepts whose powerfulness depends upon their detachment from direct experience'. The challenge for those involved in early years therefore is to:

- introduce language to children, through direct hands on experiences;
- move children on so that they use the language in a wider range of contexts, and;
- develop depth of language use and understanding that is conceptually based and where children are able to link ideas and experiences to more complex situations and ideas that are removed in terms of time and space.

Some of this development is not evident until later years, when for example, children apply scientific concepts to complex simulations, collect, store and analyse data on spreadsheets. However, the foundations are laid in the early years experiences of linking science and ICT.

Sensors

Sensors are a good example of an ICT application in science that could and should be used in early years science. Many young children do not meet sensors in science until after the age of seven or eight. Yet there are sound reasons why they should be used with young children. Let's consider the teaching of the scientific concept of temperature with young children. This is not an easy concept; young children find it difficult to equate number values to experiences of hot and cold. The standard thermometers (including those developed as 'infant thermometers') used to measure temperature do not readily assist children in developing their understanding. Thermometers have inherent difficulties and present a range of problems for upper primary children, let alone those in early years. For example:

- the spirit in the thermometer is slow to show;
- young children find the numbers difficult to read and understand;
- most scales are too small for children to read easily and with confidence;
- children are unable to equate the temperature reading with the experience of 'feeling' the temperature.

The same applies to using other sensors such as sound and light, similar problems arise using conventional equipment. However, using computer sensors with young children offers a range of advantages, which include:

- children can relate the number value to what is happening;
- readings are displayed immediately;
- children can change the environment, e.g. place the temperature sensor into ice, shout into the sound sensor, place the light sensor under their jumper, and see the change in the reading. Therefore allowing them to manipulate their environment and relate cause and effect immediately;
- a real time graph can be created and children can make changes to the environment and see what happens to the graph. This provides an opportunity for work on predictions;
- sensors are robust pieces of equipment and not easily broken;
- sensors are motivating, they are exciting pieces of equipment and intrinsically interesting, children also have a sense of 'being grown up' when using them.

Young children can learn to use sensors and work independently if provided with appropriate teaching and learning opportunities that include time for them to 'explore' using the sensors.

What should not be underestimated is children's ability to explore and as a result learn how to use sensors (and indeed other items of equipment). Children will need some 'direct teaching' to cover fundamental issues and safety and care, however children very quickly become expert. If allowed to take on the role of teacher and engage in peer tutoring they often 'volunteer' to teach interested adults, illustrating how motivation, confidence and an environment supportive of children taking the lead, can allow a role change in the classroom.

Digital cameras

Perhaps more than any other area of the curriculum, science offers the widest range of contexts for using ICT. Many of the applications, such as sensors, allow children to manipulate measurement in a way that conventional methods do not. Sensors can provide a stimulus for exploration and children delight at creating extremes, for example, making a loud noise so that the graph will show a peak or whispering to create the opposite effect. The Intel Play Computer Microscope (a focus of discussion later in this chapter) offers children views of everyday objects that are unavailable to the naked eye, often making the mundane appear fantastic.

This chapter is based on the premise that one of the key roles of ICT in primary science is to encourage children to become independent and active participants in their own learning. This includes children making decisions on what equipment to use, when to use it and, for purposes of their own choice.

The use of the digital camera is an excellent example of ICT equipment that can offer children a high level of independence. While many teachers are nervous about allowing children to use equipment worth several hundred pounds I have yet to meet a class where a child has dropped or damaged a camera! Quite the opposite: where children are allowed to use a camera they do so with care, eagerness and an eye for what is important to them.

Pedagogically there are many reasons for developing children's ability to use this piece of equipment in the early years. The digital camera offers children an immediate record of what they are observing, and the opportunity to change the view if their attempt to take the photograph is not successful. So children can practise taking photographs without 'wasting film' thus developing proficiency in an inexpensive and immediate way.

As children develop their personal expertise in using the digital camera it then offers the children a range of advantages. Feasey and Gallear (2001) suggest that children are able to:

- record immediately their experiences and phenomena;
- take photographs in their own environment when it is appropriate to them;
- check their own photographs and retake;
- view their photographs on the computer screen;
- print out photographs almost immediately rather than have to wait for film to be processed.

This sits well with the idea of learning dispositions and children being 'ready, willing and able' to engage with their own learning in contexts that are appropriate.

In relation to the development of science skills and understandings the digital camera supports the development of scientific concepts in a variety of ways. Children can take photographs of:

- children carrying out science activities;
- the equipment they use;
- different parts of their activity;
- sequences;
- change, e.g. when cooking, growing plants;
- cause and effect;
- modelling an idea;
- habitats;
- animals;
- concepts in action, e.g. playground and forces;
- seasonal change;
- changes in themselves.

The real challenge though, is not in teaching children to use ICT equipment but to develop an environment where children can access such equipment on their own terms. Of course guidance will be needed, teachers will have to scaffold children's learning and provide explicit opportunities and prompts to encourage children to use such equipment. Support will also be required to store photographs whether as a class book with scribed, written comments from individuals or as a personal book which allows children to locate important experiences which becomes part of their own learning story (an idea based on the New Zealand approach where children participate in documenting their own learning experiences (Carr 2001)). The latter is undoubtedly the ultimate goal for those involved in early years learning.

The Intel Play QXA Computer Microscope

The final ICT application in early years science under consideration is the Intel Play QXA Computer Microscope, which was given to all schools in England, as part of the Year of Science. In 2002 BECTA commissioned a team from Northumbria University to carry out a research project into the use of the Intel Microscope in primary schools in the north-east of England. The researchers worked with teachers and children from nursery through to Year 6, mainly in science lessons, although some teachers used the Intel in language and art lessons. The research findings raise a number of issues for the role of ICT in science.

The research report indicated that in the majority of schools the Intel Microscope had not been taken out of the box, indeed one school tried to return it, believing its delivery to be a clerical error. Where the Intel had been taken out of the box, use was limited and teachers only started to use it when involved in the research project. Most teachers stated that time was the key factor, they did not feel that they had sufficient time to familiarise themselves with the equipment and therefore had limited understanding of its potential.

By the end of the project, the situation was very different, teachers were enthusiastic and considered building it not only into science across the school but also into literacy sessions to support the development of written language, speaking and listening. It was the children who had used the Intel who became the computer microscope's most convincing ambassadors using adjectives to describe using it, such as 'ace', 'brilliant' and 'wicked'.

The Intel research illustrated how quickly new ICT equipment can become the norm in a classroom and how, given the right environment, children can lead learning and development in using new equipment. More importantly, children and teachers can start from almost the same knowledge base and become 'companion' learners, supporting each other. The research findings showed that the preferred learning style for finding out how the Intel Microscope worked was the same for both teachers and the children. Both engaged in 'exploration', trying things out to see how it worked. Many teachers took the Intel Microscope home and admitted to 'playing' with it, and announced that: 'I did exactly the same as the children did, I even looked at my skin, eyes, etc. just like the children' (Feasey et al. 2003: 18).

The report stated that:

> The majority of pupils became proficient in using the Intel Microscope very quickly and were keen to explore the different facilities and also to teach other children how to use the microscope. It was often the children who became the instigators of using the microscope, frequently suggesting to the teacher that they should use the microscope to view new items or use one of the numerous facilities. The children had the confidence to explore the potential of the Intel Microscope and often carried the teacher along with them. In discussions with children, it became obvious the children soon became experts in the classroom in the use of the Intel Microscope.
>
> (Feasey et al. 2003: 30)

The teachers engaged in the research were surprised to find that the children who used the Intel Microscope became highly motivated, not only in using the microscope but also in their willingness to discuss their observations and engage other people in conversation. The following is an extract from a teacher's log:

> Children were animated in their discussion with their peers; children sought an audience, to show them what they could see using the computer microscope; children were so excited about their observations that even the quietest and those with special needs engaged in conversation at a level that was above the norm for those children; the range of language used by all children, including EAL children and those with special needs was of a higher quality than usual.

Teachers were asked why they thought the Intel Microscope encouraged these kinds of responses from the children; they suggested that:

- children were highly motivated by what they could see;
- the microscope allowed them to observe things that could not be seen with the naked eye;
- observations of everyday objects were 'different' under the microscope;
- showing the views on screen or smart board, allowed children to share their reactions, ideas and comments;
- there was a 'wow' factor, which clearly motivated children.

One interesting comment from a teacher was that introducing this piece of equipment that was new to everyone, including the teacher, meant that everyone began from the same starting point; everyone was part of a learning partnership. What is clear is that new and interesting equipment that children can access in science, supports the development of positive learning dispositions and can encourage and develop independence in children.

The research showed that very young children found the microscope difficult to use unaided, but enjoyed viewing objects with the aid of an 'interested' adult. 'Children were quick to recognise some of the inherent difficulties in using the Intel Microscope . . . Getting it to focus was hard for me.' Feasey et al. (2003: 31). Older early years children were able to use the microscope independently and teachers found different ways of using images from the microscope in activities with the children.

Summary

The central premise of early years education is developing the whole child. In order to do this, teachers and other adults working with young children need to appreciate the dilemmas that individual learning situations raise. In early years science one of the greatest conflicts is between the adult teaching and the child learning at their own pace and in relation to their own interests. We must not underestimate the ability of young children to be independent learners and make decisions and take control of their environment. ICT in science allows children to do this and, where successful, helps to build positive learning dispositions which become the foundation for successful and confident learners in early years.

References

Carr, M. (2001) *Assessment in Early Childhood Settings: Learning Stories*. London: Paul Chapman Publishing.
Claxton, G. (1990) *Teaching to Learn*. London: Cassell.
De Boo, M. (2000) *Science 3 – 6 Laying the foundations in the early years*. Hatfield: ASE.
Desforges, C.W. (ed.) (1989) Early childhood education. *The British Journal of Education Psychology*, Monograph series no. 4.
Feasey, R., Gair, J. and Shaw, P. (2003) Evaluation of the Intel Play QX3 Microscope, Report to BECTA.
Feasey, R. and Gallear, B. (2001) *Primary Science and ICT*. Hatfield: ASE.
Frost, R. (1995) *IT in primary Science*. London: IT in Science Publishers.
Goodnow, J. (1990) The socialisation of cognition: What's involved? In J.W. Stigler, R.A. Shweder and G. Herdt (eds) *Cultural Psychology*, pp. 259–86. Cambridge: Cambridge University Press.
Katz, L.G. (1988) What should young children be doing? *American Educator*, (Summer): 29–45.
Siraj-Blatchford, J. and Siraj-Blatchford, I. (1995) *Educating the whole child: cross-curricular Skills, Themes and Dimensions*. Buckingham: Open University Press.

6

CREATIVITY, PROBLEM-SOLVING AND PLAYFUL USES OF TECHNOLOGY: GAMES AND SIMULATIONS IN THE EARLY YEARS

David Whitebread

In this chapter I want to argue that information and communications technology (ICT), used well, is perhaps uniquely placed to make an important contribution to developing young children's thinking. More particularly, it can help develop and nourish their creativity and their confidence as thinkers, learners and problem solvers.

The important role of creative and problem-solving approaches across the early years and primary curriculum has been widely recognised and accepted for many years (Fisher 1987, 1990; De Boo 1999; Craft 2000). In order for computer-based technology to make a contribution in this area, it needs to be used by young children in ways which recognise how they learn most effectively, and what is involved in helping them to become confident and creative thinkers. In this context, I want to suggest that children need to play with technology and, as part of this, that what are commonly referred to as 'adventure games' and simulations of various kinds, can make a particularly significant contribution.

The chapter is in two parts. The first part attempts to define the essential characteristics of a computer-based adventure game, or simulation, and discuss the ways in which they might usefully vary to provide progression and a range of different challenges. The second part of the chapter reviews some key ideas in what we currently understand from developmental psychology (exciting recent work in early brain development) about young children's learning. Throughout both parts, implications are drawn for the ways in which computer technology, adventure games and simulations in particular, can be used to most effectively support children's learning.

Characteristics of adventure games and simulations

There are a number of ways in which the essential features of adventure games and simulations could be categorised and described. The most helpful way, however, in relation to analysing games and simulations for their educational potential, is to look at the range of problem-solving skills they require for successful solution. A well constructed adventure game or simulation will incorporate all or some of the following problem-solving skills:

- understanding and representing the problem (including identifying what kinds of information are relevant to its solution);
- gathering and organizing relevant information;
- constructing and managing a plan of action, or a strategy;
- reasoning, hypothesis testing and decision making;
- using various problem-solving tools.

Understanding and representing the problem

Research has clearly established that the ways in which a problem is understood and mentally 'represented' has a major effect on the creativity of the problem solver's approaches to it and, the likelihood of it being solved. Three characteristics of games and simulations are helpful in relation to this issue, mostly by helping young children to see what is relevant and what is irrelevant to problem solution.

First, the problems are embedded in 'meaningful' contexts. Rather than being faced with arid and obviously artificial problems of the 'if two men can dig a hole in three days' variety, children playing adventure games become involved in a compelling story with goodies and baddies, with crises, setbacks, triumphs and, eventually, a satisfyingly happy ending. The children are involved in the adventure because they alone can help the King and Queen find their lost children, or they alone can save the planet, or help 'Darryl the Dragon' find the items he needs to make his breath fiery again. Such fictional contexts make these games highly motivating, because they imbue the problems contained within them with real human motivations and purposes. They also help children understand the nature and meaning of the problems, and thus enable them to maximise the use of their reasoning powers and learn from the experience more effectively.

Adventure games and simulations are also essentially, of course, highly simplified models of real world problems, and it is this simplification which is the second important characteristic. In the same way that the simplified way in which we talk to young children (sometimes referred to as 'motherese') is an enormously powerful support to their language learning, simplifying and 'cleaning up' problems clearly helps young children to see their significant features. Some readers may share my own memory of failing to solve problems in chemistry lessons because impurities in the materials or inaccuracies in my procedures caused subsidiary reactions to take place which masked the main reaction I was meant to be discovering or examining. My hydrogen would never 'pop' when ignited with a lighted spill at the end of the test tube because it had already recombined with other chemicals, which shouldn't have been there, half way up the tube. The skill in constructing a simulated problem or adventure is, therefore, to distil some important relationships from the real world so that the problem is now more easily seen, while remaining realistic and credible. This is largely a matter of making the consequences of particular decisions or actions direct and clear, which relates to the important issue of feedback in learning.

The third characteristic of games and simulations which helps young children to represent and understand problems, is that the same kinds of problems are posed in a variety of different contexts. With some adventure games, this feature is built in. For example, there are games where children solve a series of problems by writing progressively more sophisticated Logo 'programs'. Instead of just moving a screen turtle around a blank screen, however, the children are engaged in guiding a robot through a temple maze, reconnecting broken wires in a control box, mending rope bridges and so on. All these problems look very different, but have the same underlying structure (see Figure 6.1).

The same progression of developing similar problem-solving skills, but in different contexts, can be achieved by using different games with the same underlying structure. This is relatively easy to achieve because there are a number of basic structures common to many adventure games. For example, there are several games at different levels of difficulty which are essentially sequencing problems placed in the context of a search. You are searching for an object in an environment consisting of different rooms or locations. In order to do this you must go into the rooms in the correct sequence, sometimes to acquire the magic key or discover a password that you will need later. At each stage you must make the correct decisions about which way to go, whether to take the apple, what to throw at the snake, and so on. If you get the sequence wrong the Witch catches you or, you crash your land cruiser and you go back to the beginning again. Giving children the experience of applying skills and ideas they have

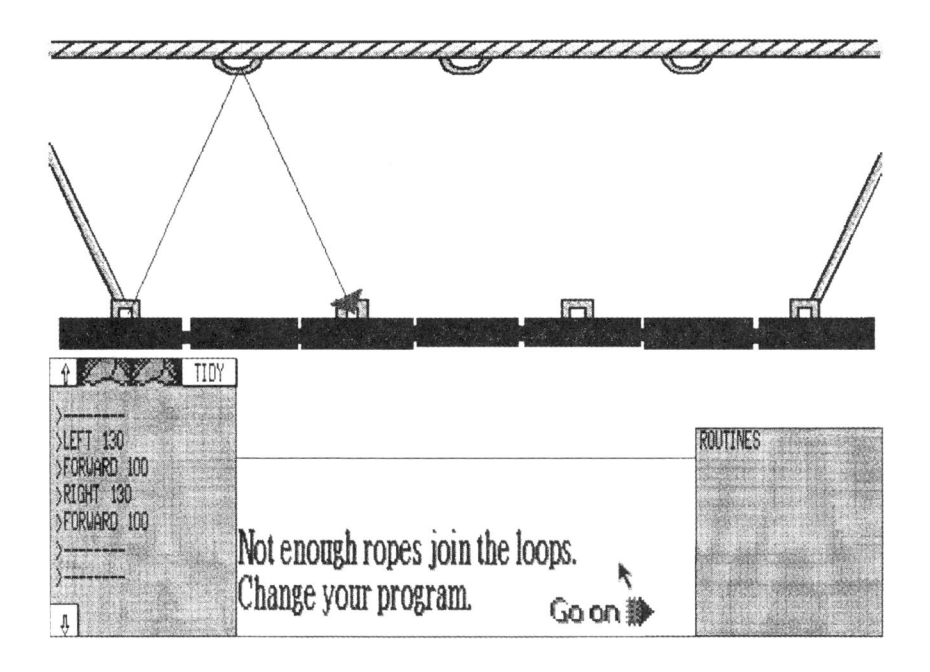

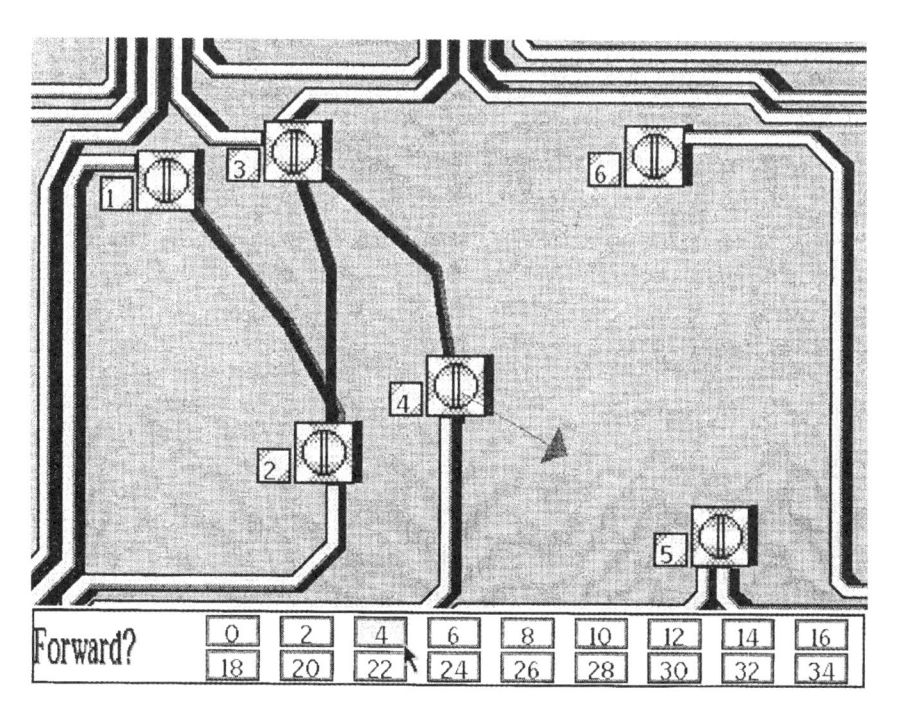

Figure 6.1 Logo problems from *Crystal Rain Forest*

learnt in one context to a new context which is superficially very different is enormously beneficial in helping them to learn how to tackle new problems. They learn to look for analogous problems they have encountered before, or things they know about which might be relevant. They also learn to analyse problems in terms of their underlying structure rather than their superficial characteristics.

Gathering and organising information

Very much part of understanding the nature of a problem is recognizing what information is relevant to its solution. The essence of many real world problems is a lack of information. Children need to develop the skills of gathering relevant information and of organizing it in ways which will help them solve problems.

Once again, this is a central feature of many adventure games. At its simplest, this may consist of being presented with particular pieces of information quite explicitly and being told you need to remember this. It might be a password to get on to the next stage of the adventure or information about the effects of different kinds of magical spells you can use when faced with particular problems. Typing 'WHOOSH' into the computer at the right moment can make you invisible and help you get past the evil Troll!

At a more advanced stage, information is discovered in different locations and needs to be remembered and used to construct increasingly complex series of moves and actions. This is where children are being required to become aware of the information they need and to search for it systematically. For example, they may discover that they cannot enter the Wizard's house because they do not have the golden key. When they find the Goblin with the golden key, he will only give it to them in exchange for a bag of corn, and so on. Gradually, as more information is collected it is constructed into a sequence of moves. When all the information is in place and correctly organised, the problem can be solved, the lost princess is found, and good triumphs over evil yet again.

The range of information presented and the length and complexity of the sequence which needs to be constructed are obvious sources of progression in this kind of game. Another source of progression is the proportion of the information presented which is irrelevant to problem solution. In less challenging games the only information available is that which is needed to solve the problem. In more challenging versions, an increasing proportion of the information presented is actually irrelevant.

There is a special kind of software which may not seem to fall into the category of 'adventure game', but which should be included because it shares a number of key features, and particularly in relation to this issue of gathering and organising relevant information. These pieces of simulation software are actually just databases constructed as hypertexts, but they are set up so that the front end or user interface presents the data in an imaginative or 'real world' context within which each user has their own unique adventure. Such a program might, for example, present data on the events in a house over a calendar year by enabling you to set the date and time and then explore the house, or it might present natural environments within which you can go on a simulated nature walk or field study, equipped with a notebook into which you can paste text and a camera with which you can take snapshot pictures of discovered flora and fauna.

The advantage for the teacher of this kind of simulation database is that problems to be solved can be constructed by the user, rather than being predetermined by the software writers of the adventure game. There is also total freedom in terms of the order in which the problem solver views and collects information. Simpler and more complex questions and challenges can therefore be set. Different problems can be devised which require different and progressively more sophisticated search strategies for relevant information. In one such program, which presents data on the events in a household over a year, one particularly exciting event is the arrival of a new baby. A whole range of different kinds of questions might be posed, each requiring a different search strategy, thus:

- What special event takes place on 3rd February? Find out as much as you can about this event.
- What begins to happen at one end of the bedroom on 21st January? Why does this happen?
- What is the Baby's typical daily routine in July, and how is it different in October? Why do you think it changes?
- Where does the Baby sleep in the afternoon, and for how long? Does the Baby always sleep in the same place in the afternoons?

To answer some of these questions you have to start at a particular date and search the whole house. For others, you can start in a particular room. Some require you to go through the whole day, while for others you can concentrate on particular times. Some answers require only a limited number of pieces of information to be collected, while much more is needed for others.

In terms of children learning to distinguish relevant and irrelevant information in relation to any particular problem, and of devising strategies for collecting relevant information, these programs therefore have a particular value.

Planning and strategies

The third characteristic of adventure games and simulations is that they require the problem solver to construct plans and devise strategies. We have already discussed above the common structure of many games which essentially involve discovering a successful sequence of moves through an environment which will reveal the necessary information and objects in the right order to allow problem solution. This is pure planning.

Children's planning abilities develop in two ways. First, they become able to construct and carry out plans which contain longer strings of 'moves' or elements. Second, their plans become more complex in structure, progressively containing subgoals, subroutines and strategies developed in other contexts and applied to the new problem. For example, it is sometimes necessary to take an action which appears to be moving you further away from the problem goal or solution, but is actually necessary to set up a situation from which you can proceed to a final solution. The classic problem of getting a dog, a cat and a mouse over a river using a boat that will only hold two of them at once is a case in point. The key move, which young children find very difficult, is to bring the cat back across the river to the starting point. Adventure games almost always require children to tackle these kinds of sequencing problems which are enormously beneficial in developing their abilities to construct plans.

A different challenge is imposed in another type of program where a sequence of moves has to be constructed and carried out under time pressure. This kind of program is sometimes dismissed as just an 'arcade' game, but it could not be more different from the relatively mindless 'splat the Aliens' type of program usually implied by this term. In these kinds of strategy games each level sets the user a new challenge, and each new challenge is a mini-adventure in itself. Often these games involve moving a creature, or group of creatures, through different environments. At the beginning relatively simple environments are used to introduce simple strategies, such as digging a hole or building a bridge, but as the game progresses the environments become increasingly challenging requiring combinations of previous strategies. Thus in one such game a strategy for long drops where there is solid ground at the bottom, involves parachuting a creature down, turning him around (which involves parachuting a second creature down and turning him into a 'blocker') and then transforming the first creature into a builder to build a ladder back up, which the other creatures can then walk down. This would not be such a useful strategy, however, for a long drop with water at the bottom. This needs a different strategy, probably involving digging down diagonally through the cliff, coming out near the bottom and then building a bridge from there. The range of possible combinations of the different possible actions means that many different strategies can be constructed, and many problems can be solved in a number of different ways.

What we see in all this is the opportunity for children to practise a number of key problem-solving skills. They are devising strategies which they then have to apply appropriately in different contexts and which they have to adapt and co-ordinate together to build a plan of action. The computer-based adventure game context is a powerful tool for learning these skills because it provides motivation and, to a probably unique extent, the opportunity for rapid trial and error learning.

With computers, children are peculiarly free to make mistakes, to redo things, to try things in different ways which they are perhaps not so free to do in other media. I was first alerted to the particular strength of computers in this area when working with young children using a computer graphics program. At the press of a key the child could rub out anything they didn't like (and without making a nasty smudge or a hole in the paper!) they could change the thickness of a line, or the colour of a shape, and so on. The opportunities for experimentation were boundless in a way that paint, chalk or crayon cannot really offer to a young child. The same is very much the case with problem-solving. In an adventure game, you can try out one possibility, see that it doesn't work, and try out another, all in a matter of moments. In real, practical problem-solving in mathematics, science or design technology it is very much more difficult to provide for this kind of trial and error learning. In practical work children can very easily spend a lot of time and effort on an idea before it becomes clear to them that it will not work. In an adventure game probably the worst that can happen is that you are splatted by the Aliens, or eaten by the wicked Witch, but you always miraculously survive to have another go, and you have learned what not to do the next time!

Reasoning, hypothesis testing and decision making

Well constructed adventure games and simulations provide a wealth of opportunities for children to practise the skills of reasoning, hypothesis testing and decision making. At the simplest level, this can be a matter of making decisions about which direction to choose for the next move. If we chose to go north last time we reached this point, and were faced with a dead end, or a fearsome monster, then we might deduce that going south this time might be worth trying. In this instance, the children are being asked to apply knowledge gained about the particular adventure. In other games and simulations, however, opportunities are provided for the children to apply their real world knowledge to a problem, such as when they are asked which piece of equipment they wish to use to help them solve a particular problem, or which items they wish to take on their journey that might potentially be useful.

Different kinds of adventure games provide opportunities for different kinds of reasoning. The kind of adventure game which is essentially concerned with constructing a sequence of moves involves the children in making predictions about what will happen next if a particular move is made. Thus, the children make hypotheses and then test them. In one such game drinking a potion of a particular colour makes you invisible.

The children might then predict that they will at last be able to get past the Troll who is guarding the trapdoor, and so it turns out!

The kind of games which involve exploring, what we have referred to earlier as simulation databases, lend themselves more to making inferences. Thus, in the simulation database we discussed earlier of the events in a household over a year, partly because you only see static 'snapshots' of the various rooms of the house, you have to make inferences about events largely from the changing location of objects. Thus, the Baby's daily routine in its early months can be partly inferred from the location of the pram, which is in the hall when the Baby is in the cot, outside in the garden when it contains the Baby, and nowhere to be seen when the Baby has gone shopping with Mum.

Other simulations are set up to model cause and effect relationships and involve children in making decisions and learning about the significance of different factors from the consequences. A relatively simple example models a seaside teashop, where you have to decide how many ice creams and cups of tea to prepare each day, based on weather forecasts. More advanced programs, where the cause and effect relationships are more complex, model the ecology of a pond (where you can add different plants and animals), the planning of a town or city, and the design of a Grand Prix racing car.

Clearly, such programs provide plentiful opportunities for reasoning and discussion. Indeed a good criteria for assessing the educational value of computer games and simulations might well be the amount of discussion which they generate. Such programs can thus encourage skills of verbal expression and articulation as well as those of pure reasoning.

Using problem-solving tools

The final characteristic of adventure games and simulations is that they involve children in the use of a range of problem-solving tools. Essentially, these consist of ways of recording information and constructing plans when problems become complicated and too difficult to manage just in our heads. They might consist of notes, diagrams, measurements, maps, scale models and so on.

Many adventure games make use of maps (Figure 6.2 contains some examples). Some provide a map on screen, others gradually reveal the map as different areas are explored and others involve the exploration of an environment, but do not offer a map as such within the program. Quite a useful progression is clearly to give children the experience of using a program with a map, and then helping them to construct their own map of an environment for which one is not provided.

The use of drawings and models in problem-solving is an important and perhaps under-taught skill in the early years and primary schooling. Research related to children's drawings (Thomas and Silk 1990; Cox 1992)

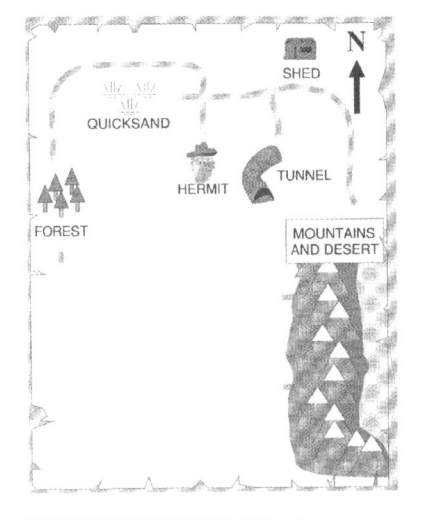

Dinosaur Discovery

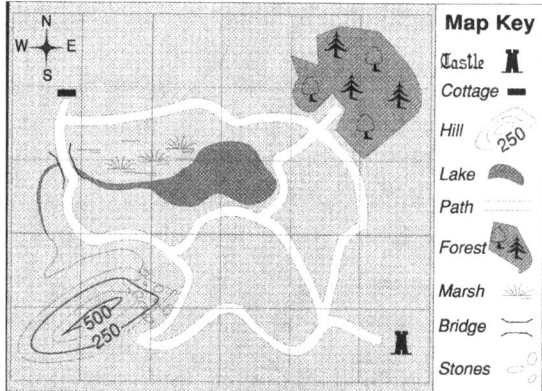

Granny's Garden

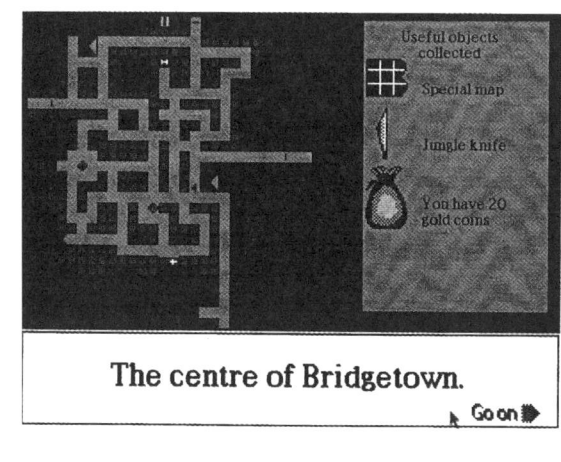

Crystal Rain Forest

Figure 6.2 Adventure game maps

has shown that children naturally draw about what they know, partly to help them represent and understand their experiences. This is an important element in children's learning which can usefully be encouraged and developed through the use of adventure games and simulations.

Children's learning, ICT and adventure games

It is clear from this review of the essential characteristics of educationally valuable adventure games and simulations, that they have much to offer in relation to the development of children's abilities as creative problem solvers.

Like any other educational resource, however, it is important for the teacher to understand how to use it to maximum effect. This second part of the chapter, therefore, reviews some key elements in what we know currently about the development of children's thinking and explores the ways ICT, and adventure games and simulations in particular, can make a contribution to this. This gives us clear guidelines as to the ways to use this kind of computer software with young children if it is to make a real contribution to developing children's creative thinking and problem-solving abilities.

This part of the chapter is divided into two sections. The first section reviews current evidence about how children learn to be creative problem solvers, and the overwhelming significance of play within these learning processes. The second section reviews the key developments in children's learning and thinking. In both sections the implications for the contribution of ICT, and particularly adventure games and simulations is also explored.

How children learn to be creative problem solvers: the significance of play

Any review of children's learning has to begin with the work of Piaget who revolutionised the way psychologists and teachers think about this area. Perhaps the most significant contribution made by Piaget, however, was the establishment of the idea that children are active thinkers who learn by constructing their own understandings. Learning is thus seen as an essentially creative process. The example is often quoted of the way in which children learn language. They do not simply imitate and repeat what they hear in adult language, but typically produce a constant stream of completely novel utterances (in my family we even have words and whole phrases which we now all use, but which were originally invented by the children). Many of these novel words and phrases that children produce, furthermore, are clearly the consequence of misapplying patterns and rules which they have constructed for themselves. For example, you will hear young children say that yesterday they 'goed to the shops and buyed something'. They will not have heard an adult say this; nor has any adult taught them that you create the past tense by adding on 'ed'.

In fact, what emerges from a wide range of recent and contemporary research is that children learn predominantly by processes of induction and analogy. This involves detecting patterns or regularities within the variety of their experience; neuroscientific evidence has also confirmed that it is this kind of process for which the human brain seems to be peculiarly well adapted. In the case of language learning discussed above, children detect patterns and regularities from the huge variety of their experience of spoken English. Within the brain, learning has been shown to be a process of making new connections between neurones and building up ever more complex neuronal networks. As it turns out, this understanding of the nature of human learning has confirmed the fundamental importance of play.

Psychologists have been researching and developing theories about the nature and purposes of children's play since the middle of the 19th century. It has been suggested as a mechanism for letting off steam, providing relaxation, relieving boredom, practising for adult life, living out our fantasies and many more. That it is important in children's development, however, has never been in doubt. As Moyles (1989) demonstrated, for every aspect of human development and functioning, there is a form of play.

It is only in the last 20–30 years, however, that the brain's significance for thinking, problem-solving and creativity has been fully recognised. Bruner (1972), in a famous article entitled 'The nature and uses of immaturity', is generally credited with first pointing out to psychologists and educationalists the relationship across different animal species between the capacity for learning and the length of immaturity, or dependence upon adults. He also pointed out that as the period of immaturity lengthens, so does the extent to which the young are playful. He argued that play is one of the key experiences through which young animals learn, and also the means by which their intellectual abilities themselves are developed.

The human being, of course, has a much greater length of immaturity than any other animal, plays more and for longer, and is supreme, of course, in flexibility of thought. Play is significant in this, Bruner argues, because it provides opportunities to try out possibilities, to put different elements of a situation together in various ways, to look at problems from different viewpoints. This accords very closely to Craft's (2000) recent definition of creativity as 'possibility thinking'. In this excellent book, Craft demonstrates that creativity in this sense is not, as it is often conceived, a process confined to the arts but, a fundamental aspect of human learning, properly applicable across the curriculum.

Bruner demonstrated this relation between play, creativity and problem-solving in a series of experiments (Sylva et al. 1976) where children were asked to solve practical problems. Typically in these experiments, one group of children was given the opportunity to play with the objects involved, while the other group was 'taught' how to use the objects in ways which would help solve the problem. Consistently, the 'play' group subsequently outperformed the 'taught' group when they were then left alone to tackle the problem. The children who had the experience of playing with the materials were more inventive in devising strategies to solve the problem, they persevered longer when their initial attempts did not work and so, not surprisingly, were more successful in their attempts to solve the problem.

As a consequence of the freedom it offers to try things out, change things, etc., ICT offers particularly powerful opportunities to be playful in the way that Bruner has described. Only recently, we were working with some 3-year-olds on a program which required them to enter their names. They were quite interested to see what their name looked like on the computer, but they were thrilled to discover that if you hold you finger down on a key the computer produces an endless stream of letters. And, if you then hold your finger down on the delete key they all disappear again! This discovery produced endless mirth and what seemed like hours of fun. Along the same lines is children's consistent delight, which I have observed repeatedly, in deliberately pressing the wrong button, or giving the wrong answer, to see what will happen. This playful approach is very much to be encouraged and enjoyed within the context of adventures and simulations. Children who are allowed to play around with these games and explore different possibilities will be much more creative and effective in solving any problems posed.

Observation of children at play gives some indication of why it might be such a powerful learning medium. During play children are usually totally engrossed in what they are doing. It is quite often repetitive and contains a strong element of practice. During play children set their own level of challenge, and so what they are doing is always developmentally appropriate (to a degree which tasks set by adults will never be). Play is spontaneous and initiated by the children themselves; in other words, during play children are in control of their own learning.

Guha (1987) has argued that this last element is particularly significant. There are many examples in psychological research of tasks where being in control has turned out to be crucial for effective learning. Guha cites, for example, experiments concerned with visual learning in which subjects are required to wear 'goggles' which make everything look upside down. They are then required to sit in a wheelchair and learn to move safely through an environment. The results of such experiments show that subjects moving themselves around the environment (and having a lot of initial 'crashes') learn to do this much more quickly than those who are wheeled safely about by an adult helper. The parallels here with Bruner's play groups and taught groups is striking.

This issue of control also relates strongly to two further important ideas in children's learning, namely responsiveness and confidence. We have all had the experience of the young infant who delights in repetitive play, where they throw an object on the floor and the adult picks it up, over and over again, with the child's glee becoming more and more unbounded (unlike the adult's). It has been very clearly established from a whole range of research (originally responding to Bowlby's work on child care) that young children flourish best when their adult carers are responsive and where their experience is consistent and predictable (Schaffer 1977). This same principle was demonstrated quite a long time ago by an unexpected finding from Watson and Ramey's (1972) 'contingency mobile' experiment. This involved families with 8-week-old infants using a special cot onto which was joined a mobile. When the mobile moved it proved to be no more interesting to the infants than if it stayed still. However, if the mobile moved when the infant pressed down on the pillow, this became hugely fascinating and the research team had some difficulty in retrieving their apparatus at the end of the experiment! These infants were in control and their parents could see for themselves the huge benefits this brought to their child's wellbeing.

Because of the responsive and interactive nature of ICT (and adventure games in particular) the computer itself is capable of providing feedback, help and support to children. While they may still need some guidance occasionally from the teacher, this need is often much reduced by the use of software which can react contingently dependent upon the child's behaviour (a feature which, of course, makes playing adventure games highly motivating). This strongly supports the child's sense of being in control, and of independence in their learning.

It is clearly important for the teacher to be sensitive to these issues. In relation to adventures and simulations it might imply allowing children to set their own challenges and tackling them in their own way. In my experience, it is also important to allow children to revisit games: just as they love hearing the same story endlessly repeated, they love revisiting well loved games or parts of games. Adults are often irritated by games which make them go back to the beginning and repeat already worked out moves, but this is rarely the case with young children. On the contrary, this kind of repetition seems to contribute to their enjoyment of the game, probably because it is increasing their sense of familiarity and control.

What emerges from a wide range of research over the past 20–30 years, is that children learn to be confident and flexible thinkers when they grow up in an environment which is responsive, consistent and encourages them to be playful. They need to be in control of their own learning and will learn most powerfully through tackling real and meaningful problems in their own ways, rather than by being 'taught' set procedures.

How children's thinking develops

Children are, of course, often quite ingenious in their problem-solving abilities and highly original and creative – you only have to watch them at play on a computer game, effortlessly outscoring their olders and betters, or at play making up mythical adventures, inventing extraordinary games or building their own weird inventions and contraptions to realise that. Yet it is also clear that there are, in fact, huge individual differences in these kinds of highly valued abilities. It is also clear that teachers can have a very powerful role in either encouraging and stimulating this kind of mental activity or, sadly, in discouraging and extinguishing it.

In an exhaustive review of research Sternberg and Powell (1983) pinpointed the key developments in children's learning and thinking which are now generally accepted among developmental psychologists. According to this analysis, as they develop children become:

- more exhaustive in their information processing;
- more able to comprehend relations of successively higher orders;
- more flexible in their use of strategies and information;
- more sophisticated in their reflections upon and control of their own thinking.

Let us, briefly, take the various points in turn and look at their implications for the use of ICT, particularly adventure games and simulations.

More exhaustive information processing

Children and adults who are better problem solvers have been found to engage in more exhaustive processing of all relevant information and consequently to spend longer encoding and representing problems to themselves before they start out on a solution (Sternberg and Rifkin 1979). Young children tend to be impulsive and to respond too quickly to a situation or problem before they have had chance to assimilate all the relevant information. We will all have experienced the tendency of young children to do this. Sometimes when being given instructions about a new task they rush off (out of pure excitement!) and then have to come back to find out what it was exactly that they had to do. There are also, however, considerable individual differences in this area of 'cognitive tempo' and these can have important consequences for children's learning. Borkowski et al. (1983), for example, demonstrated significant relationships between impulsivity–reflectivity, metamemory, strategy use and performance on a range of memory tasks.

In the light of this kind of evidence, it is perhaps worth reflecting on the balance which is struck in many primary school classrooms between encouraging children to get on quickly and complete tasks and then to take time to reflect carefully and systematically upon the task before attempting it. As we have seen, computer-based adventure games and simulations are very well designed to encourage children to be more systematic in the gathering of information. As teachers, it is well worth encouraging this element of problem-solving.

The ability to comprehend relations of successively higher orders

There is also a clear and well documented progression in children's thinking from being only able to consider the particular task, problem, object or incident at hand to being able to consider issues at a more abstract level, where a range of different instances might be taken on board simultaneously. As the work of Donaldson (1978) and others have shown children's ability to reason is particularly context dependent. Primary school teachers are very familiar with this phenomenon: children can appear to understand an idea on one day, but then can be completely baffled by a slight change to the way it is presented on the next.

We have noted earlier that the use of powerfully 'meaningful' fictional contexts is a key element in adventure games which helps children to understand and make sense of problems. When using adventure games and simulations in the early years classroom it is, therefore, important to build on and support this characteristic. This can helpfully be done, for example, by developing a range of non-computer activities which use the same scenarios and characters and explore similar problems to those involved in the computer program (Underhay (1989) reviews some excellent projects along these lines).

The development of the ability to see relationships between different tasks would appear to be dependent upon the accumulation and continual restructuring of knowledge, driven by the processes of induction and analogy. This issue of 'transfer' is a crucial one in learning. Research reviewed by Meadows (1993) indicates that children are more likely to be able to transfer understandings or processes from one task to another where, among other things, they encounter a range of examples with a common structure but different irrelevant characteristics. As we have seen, this is another common and very valuable feature of computer-based adventure games.

The ability to deal with higher order and more abstract relationships is also dependent upon the use of language and other forms of symbolic representation. These enable information to be 'chunked' into larger units which can then be processed and manipulated more easily. The work of Vygotsky (1986) on tools, signs and symbols in the development of human thinking, and Bruner (1973) on the development of enactive, iconic and symbolic modes of representation, has been most significant in this area. Non-computer activities which require children to represent their knowledge and understandings about the scenarios, characters and problems involved in particular games are, therefore, clearly indicated.

Models can be built, drawings made, stories retold and so on, all to great benefit.

Two key aspects of the way in which language helps learning in the context of social interaction have also emerged from research stimulated by Vygotsky's and Bruner's work. First, it is clear that we come to understand ideas better through the process of articulating them in social or group problem-solving situations. As anyone who has ever taught knows, being required to explain something to someone else is often the best way to come to understand it oneself. Second, language is used in social contexts to 'scaffold', support and guide problem-solving processes and procedures. This kind of research has been partly responsible for a resurgence of interest during the last few years in the use of collaborative groupwork in primary classrooms (Dunne and Bennett 1990).

In this context, it is interesting to note that, although initially thought of in terms of individualised learning, computers have generally been used by groups in classrooms, and the view of many teachers is that learning to work in groups is one of the main advantages of computer use in schools (Jackson et al. 1986). Crook (1994) has reviewed the extensive range of work being carried out in schools involving collaborative learning with computers. Interestingly, as we noted earlier, adventure games and simulations have been found to be particularly powerful in generating collaborative talk and discussion. Organizing children into collaborative groups when they are working with adventure games and simulations is thus clearly indicated.

Flexibility in the use of strategy or information and the development of more sophisticated control strategies (metacomponents)

The last two key areas of development identified by Sternberg and Powell (1983) are very much interlinked and so we can deal with them together. We now know, through the work of neuroscientists, that unlike a computer, the human brain carries out several processes simultaneously. As a consequence, we are capable of carrying out intellectual or physical tasks and simultaneously monitoring what we are doing. That this is fundamental to human learning, has been established by a huge amount of research in the last 20 years or so concerned with the development of what have become known as 'metacognitive' processes and abilities. What emerges from this literature is a three stage process whereby we become increasingly able to construct, select and customise cognitive strategies to enable us to carry out even more different and demanding tasks with maximum mental efficiency. This process consists of:

- monitoring and evaluating our cognitive processes;
- building up metacognitive knowledge about tasks and our own intellectual processes and abilities;

- constructing and selecting even more appropriate strategies.

Developing these kinds of abilities is crucial to children's development as thinkers and learners, precisely because they enable children to take what they have learnt in one area and use it in another. A wide range of evidence has shown that it is in these abilities that many children with learning difficulties are particularly weak (Sugden 1989). As we have seen, developing and reflecting upon strategies and plans of action is a central element in many adventure games, and can also be developed through requiring children to 'interrogate' some kinds of simulations and databases.

The other point to note here is that the development of human thinking is characterised by increasing flexibility. Uniquely, as human beings, we are capable of dealing with new situations, of solving new problems and of being genuinely creative. Within neuroscience this flexibility of thought is commonly referred to as the 'plasticity' of the human brain (Greenfield 1997). We are unlike any other species in the extent that our brain grows after birth (it roughly quadruples in size in the first four years and continues growing well into our teenage years). This enables us to adapt to the circumstances in which we find ourselves, and to continue to adapt to changing circumstances, to a degree far beyond the capacity of any other species.

This growth in size is not accommodating the growth of new cells; rather it is accommodating the growth of new connections. We are born with all (or, according to the very latest research, the vast majority of) the brain cells we are ever going to have, but throughout life these cells continually form literally hundreds of thousands of connections with other cells. However, the connections made in the first few years are overwhelmingly important because they construct the basic neural architecture upon which further learning will be imposed.

This finding has contributed to the increased recognition of the importance of early years education over recent years. It has also lead to the increasing recognition of the importance of children's play for their intellectual development, as we have discussed above. Playfulness and the flexibility of thought which lead human beings to create and enjoy games, puzzles, jokes, stories and so on are not just fun, they are fundamental characteristics of the human brain and all our scientific and artistic achievements. Engaging young children in the challenges posed by computer-based adventure games can, in my view, make an important contribution to these kinds of abilities.

Conclusion

This chapter has attempted to identify the creative and problem-solving skills which can be encouraged by the use of adventure games and simulations. Based on current research evidence about the nature of children's learning, I have also tried to identify guidelines for the use of adventure games and simulations in early years and primary classrooms. It is important to do this because computers are seductive. We need to be clear about the ways in which we are using them. Asking children to do sums on the computer, and when they get them right the Duck quacks, or the Alien explodes, or whatever, seems to me to be a tragic misuse of the technology. If this is the main kind of activity which we provide with computers in early years classrooms we will have missed huge creative opportunities.

As is easily apparent, games and simulations on computers embody the general features of learning and of ICT's distinctive contribution discussed above, and often in particularly powerful ways. They encourage a playful approach to learning, they place problems in 'meaningful' contexts and they lend themselves to collaborative work and discussion. They are also stunning in their ability to engage children's interest and commitment. This is one of the real strengths of the adventure game format. By placing everything in the context of a compelling fictional world, these games are able to offer children 'off the peg' problems but in a way which makes them real and living. The one feature of adventure games that I have noticed every time I have used one with children is how involved the children have become in the story. The most successful of these games become like well loved books. The children want to play them again and again.

My own first experience of using adventure games was with an infant class using *Granny's Garden* when it first came out as a program for the BBC computer in the early 1980s. I was bowled over by the enthusiasm of the children's response. Children in this age group are, of course, very excited about fairy stories with witches and dragons and elves, and the program tapped into this area of interest very effectively (Figure 6.3). But it was the problem-solving element of the program that seemed to really enthral them. The whoops of glee when each of the lost children was discovered were electric. If all the tasks we set children in school always elicited the level of involvement and perseverance that I have consistently seen with adventure games then we would have longago said good-bye to any problems of discipline, motivation, disruption, truancy and boredom. It is my contention that this kind of computer-based creative problem-solving taps into some very essential features of young children's learning and can make a very exciting contribution to the development of young children's abilities as independent, thinking and creative problem-solvers, abilities which they will need more than ever in the twenty-first century world in which they are growing up.

Figure 6.3 The Witch from *Granny's Garden*

References

Borkowski, J.G., Peck, V.A., Reid, M.K. and Kurtz, B.E. (1983) Impulsivity and strategy transfer: Metamemory as mediator, *Child Development*, 54: 459–73.
Bruner, J.S. (1972) The nature and uses of immaturity, *American Psychologist*, 27: 1–28.
Bruner, J.S. (1973) *Beyond the Information Given*. London: George Allen and Unwin.
Cox, M. (1992) *Children's Drawings*. London: Penguin.
Craft, A. (2000) *Creativity across the Primary Curriculum*. London: Routledge.
Crook, C. (1994) *Computers and the Collaborative Experience of Learning*. London: Routledge.
De Boo, M. (1999) *Enquiring Children, Challenging Teaching*. Buckingham: Open University Press.
Donaldson, M. (1978) *Children's Minds*. London: Fontana.
Dunne, E. and Bennett, N. (1990) *Talking and Learning in Groups*. London: Macmillan.
Fisher, R. (1987) *Problem-solving in Primary Schools*. Oxford: Basil Blackwell.
Fisher, R. (1990) *Teaching Children to Think*. Oxford: Basil Blackwell.
Greenfield, S. (1997) *The Human Brain: A guided tour*. London: Weidenfeld and Nicolson.
Guha, M. (1987) Play in school, in G.M. Blenkin and A.V. Kelly (eds) *Early Childhood Education: A Developmental Curriculum*. London: Paul Chapman.

Jackson, A., Fletcher, B. and Messer, D. (1986) A survey of microcomputer use and provision in primary schools, *Journal of Computer Assisted Learning*, 2: 45–55.
Meadows, S. (1993) *The Child as Thinker*. London: Routledge.
Moyles, J.R. (1989) *Just Playing? The Role and Status of Play in Early Childhood Education*. Milton Keynes: Open University Press.
Schaffer, R. (1977) *Mothering*. London: Fontana.
Sternberg, R.J. and Powell, J.S. (1983) The development of intelligence, in P.H. Mussen, J.H. Flavell and E.M. Markman (eds) *Handbook of Child Psychology*, vol. 3. New York: Wiley.
Sternberg, R.J. and Rifkin, B. (1979) The development of analogical reasoning processes, *Journal of Experimental Child Psychology*, 27: 195–232.
Sugden, D. (1989) Skill generalisation and children with learning difficulties, in D. Sugden (ed.) *Cognitive Approaches in Special Education*. London: Falmer.
Sylva, K., Bruner, J.S. and Genova, P. (1976) The role of play in the problem-solving of children 3–5 years old, in J.S. Bruner, A. Jolly and K. Sylva (eds) *Play: Its Role in Development and Evolution*. Harmondsworth: Penguin.
Thomas, G.V. and Silk, A.M.J. (1990) *An Introduction to the Psychology of Children's Drawings*. Hemel Hempstead: Harvester Wheatsheaf.
Underhay, S. (1989) Project work: Adventure games, in R. Crompton (ed.) *Computers and the Primary Curriculum 3–13*. Lewes: Falmer Press.
Vygotsky, L.S. (1986) *Thought and Language*. Cambridge, MA: MIT Press.
Watson, J.S. and Ramey, C.T. (1972) Reactions to response-contingent stimulation in early infancy, *Merrill-Palmer Quarterly*, 18: 219–27.

7

VISUAL LITERACY AND PAINTING WITH TECHNOLOGY: OBSERVATIONS IN THE EARLY YEARS CLASSROOM

Janet Cooke and John Woollard

In this chapter we show that the effective use of information and communications technology (ICT) to enable creativity is dependent upon careful consideration of the human computer interface. Designed well, children can remember activities associated with icons and become proficient in the use of software. Less well designed icons can impede ICT based creativity and the development of ICT capability. It is also important that the ICT activities are embedded in physical experiences to ensure that the relationships between icons, functions and 'real' activities are appreciated. The underpinning research shows that there is a value in the creativity enabled by computers as well as the value in developing children's computing skills and understanding. It shows that children also begin to understand the use of icons to represent concepts in a similar way that symbols and signs represent mathematical and logic concepts in other subjects such as geography, mathematics and science. The findings also underpin the necessity and facility for teachers to evaluate software before its use in the classroom.

When a child paints, when a child draws and when a child pastes they participate in Piagetian concrete activity. The activities are concrete because they are the combination of mental processing and physical activities. On the computer the situation is similar. The extent to which ICT based painting, drawing and pasting are concrete activities is reflected in the way in which young children can learn and apply their learning with relatively little reinforcement. Our research work suggests that the icons associated with the computer activities of painting, drawing and pasting are remembered more easily than the verbal oral instructions and perhaps as easily as the practical objects themselves. The work, therefore, shows the importance of computer-based painting both in the expressive and artistic development of the child and their computer awareness and computer skills education. An important principle when we use computers with young children is that we are not simply letting them paint or draw on the computer, but we are giving them experience of computing for its own sake. That experience develops their knowledge and understanding of computing processes thus securing their future ICT capability. As we will see, that capability is dependent upon and facilitated by the use of icons to represent both virtual and physical activities.

By using a range of stimulating materials on the screen and, by giving the children opportunities to move and organise those images, we are helping to develop their visual literacy. These activities are enjoyable and educative. They remain in the concrete domain yet use tools that can equally be used to support cognitive developments. The computer can also be used to present the child with a range of images and visual devices to support pre-reading and literacy development. The means by which teachers can assess the skills, knowledge and understanding within the expressive and computer domain, are discussed along with how those skills and assessments relate to other areas of the curriculum or other aspects of education of the young child.

This chapter is in three parts. The first part describes the theoretical underpinning of learning, the association between icons and concepts and attempts to define the essential characteristics of a computer-based adventure game or simulation, and discuss the ways in which teachers might usefully vary the activities to provide progression and a range of different challenges. The second part reviews some key ideas in what we currently understand from developmental psychology (and exciting work in early brain development) about young children's learning. Throughout both parts, implications are drawn for the ways in which computer technology, and adventure games and simulations in particular, can be used to most effectively support children's learning. The third part reports upon classroom research observing young children using painting programs.

Symbolic activities and symbolic distancing

From an early age young children engage in activities which are symbolic and this is demonstrated by their use of language and in their play. From the age of 18 months children are able to create meaning in their minds and to express that meaning through gesture, language and objects. This ability to transform objects or situations through the use of imagination into meanings that are different from the original object or situation forms the foundation for intellectual development and communication. Young children's play is characterised by the use of symbols to represent objects, ideas and situations not present in the immediate time and place. Symbolic play often provides a vehicle for children to explore new concepts and experiences.

The research in this area has sought to document a sequence of progressive symbolic distancing. As children mature, they are able to use objects that are increasingly removed in form and function from the objects they wish to symbolise (Nourot and Van Hoorn 1991). Vygotsky (1978) regarded symbolic play as critical for facilitating the child's construction of a functioning symbol system and as this symbolism develops, meaning is then independent of objects so that the child can operate with more arbitrary and abstract symbols. Potter (1996) describes research where young children have been given specific play experiences to aid this process of developing symbolism. The findings of Rosen (1974) demonstrated that children given training in symbolic play developed greater skills in problem-solving and early literacy activities. Thus, symbolic play can help children move towards an understanding of more formal symbolic representation such as shapes, letters and numbers. Painting, both physical and virtual, is an important vehicle for learning and understanding. The use of the computer in the early years classroom is yet one more way in which the teacher can enrich the learning environment.

From an early age, young children are in a similar way initiated into the use of metaphor in language. Children become familiar with this symbolic use of language and appear to understand it intuitively. They meet it in everyday conversation, through riddles and word play, and it is used to communicate and develop meaning. It can be argued that although metaphor is a powerful means of communication, in order to become fully involved, it is necessary for a child to possess the knowledge needed to interpret the metaphor within its context. It is easy for metaphor to become a type of code, which can be interpreted only by those initiated into its secrets. The interpretation and use of metaphor, however, can extend the capacity to reason and think reflectively and it is important to develop this potential in children.

This study indicates that young children readily engage with symbolism in their play and language and are able to understand and use this in their activities. It is suggested by Vygotsky (1978), however, that symbolism is more easily interpreted and integrated into their understanding when it is supported through a real context and linked to existing knowledge and learning. The importance of planning the physical experiences of children before introducing virtual concepts will be shown later.

Considering metaphor and icon

The term 'metaphor' is traditionally associated with language use. When we want to convey an abstract concept in a more familiar and accessible form, we frequently resort to a metaphoric expression and we use prior knowledge to understand new situations. The interface metaphor has developed from a need to communicate the abstract concepts of a computer system and functions through concrete associations. By using real world objects to present abstract ideas, it is believed that users draw from previous learning and therefore learn more quickly and with less effort. Interface metaphors enable users to construct a mental model (Lynch 1994) and through reference to familiar habits, tasks and concrete objects, makes the abstract and invisible functions of the computer easier to understand and remember. Successful interface metaphors should be simple systems which offer consistency and do not require the user to learn and remember many rules and procedures.

Interface metaphors are increasingly becoming a prominent part of commercially available software with more generalized 'container' metaphors to represent the nature of the application. The original metaphor of the 'desktop' for business applications, such as word processors and spreadsheets, represents office objects, such as folders, clipboards, waste baskets as icons on the screen. Interface metaphors have evolved for other types of application and one good example is the art application, which uses the artist's 'canvas', a palette of colours and a range of icons to represent the drawing and painting tools available. Many of these container metaphors are becoming standardised between the different commercial versions and are beginning to offer some transferability and consistency between applications.

The graphical user interfaces developed as part of programs for children generally follow the same container metaphors as those used for adult programs. Art applications for children use a colour palette and a selection of simple painting tools. If the concept behind the use of metaphor is to enable the user to make abstract associations with concrete objects, it should follow that in order to understand and use the interface effectively, children need these concrete experiences. Importantly, teachers must be aware of the importance of the iconic representation of the concept and, help the children make the connection between the iconic image and the functionality behind the buttons.

From the iconic to the concrete

Many of the functions of an application with a graphical user interface are represented in pictorial form, as icons. Some of these are direct representations of the function, for example, a picture of a printer for 'print'. Some use metaphor to represent a more complex or abstract function, such as a picture of a pair of scissors to depict the function 'cut'. Many icons are now being generalised across applications and their functions are becoming standardised on a variety of interfaces. Most graphical user interfaces designed for adults, however, offer alternative methods of presentation in addition to the use of icons, such as menus and text labels which appear when the cursor is positioned over the icon. This additional level of support enables the user to select the method they prefer or use a combination of the two, but it is not a viable option for supporting young children with limited reading skills.

Icon and interface design are an evolving discipline which endeavour to improve human–computer interaction and usability. The organization and position of icons on the screen can be important for the user and, many applications allow the user to customise the interface to present icons in a horizontal or vertical format, change the size of the icon or remove icons (not frequently used) from the screen. 'Direct manipulation' aims to provide the user with a feeling of control over the objects they are working with and feedback to their actions. For example, when an icon is selected it will 'depress' in the same way as a button on a machine to indicate that it has been switched on. Other features of icon design, which can influence the interaction between the computer and the user, include use of colour, style of drawing, three dimensional effects and animation, and are implemented to a greater or lesser degree on the graphical user interface. It is these subtleties of action, like the depressed icon, that children need to be made aware of when introduced to the computer.

Given that icons comprise a large part of a graphical user interface and that this design method is the key approach currently adopted for applications for children, it is important to consider the nature of icons for use with young children. Jones (1993) states that icons designed for use by children should 'clearly depict, indicate and distinguish a program's commands and operations' and also 'should suggest and indicate a command intention rather than just duplicate or represent a particular pictorial form'. This is particularly important for young children who, with little or no reading skills, are not able to use the additional verbal support such as text labels, which are available to adults. The goal for educational software developers should therefore be to incorporate icons which are realistic and meaningful for children and which leave little room for misinterpretation. Jones (1993) says 'at present the iconic component in existing interfaces for children's use generally mirrors what is available in the commercial marketplace and does not respond to the developmental world of the child'. It is a difficult task to find the icon that would be representative of a concept to the whole of a learner population. Therefore, a 'best guess' icon is designed and it is for the teacher to ensure that the link between concept and image are strengthened through discussion and illustration.

Quantifying children's understanding

Our research focused upon four aspects of children's use of painting programs. At the simplest level it is the children's ability to match an icon name with the image they see. This is akin to responding 'bus' in response to a picture of a bus or 'b' in response to the letter shape b. The second aspect determined the children's ability to carry out the skill associated with the functions of the art packages. The children's ability to describe the functions of an art program simply by viewing the icon associated with it was recorded. The first activity the children were asked to do was explore the icons (tools) and talk about what they thought they would do. Their responses and questions were noted. The product of the children's art work was then considered in the light of visual literacy skills analysis. There were 52 children, aged between 4 years 10 months and 5 years 6 months, taken from three different schools in the original investigation. They were divided into two groups, which were taught differently. One group was given extra interaction away from the computer, handling 'real' objects associated with painting and the icons that are used in the computer programs. The other group were introduced straightaway to the computer painting program. A week later, the children's recollection of their understanding of the icons and functions was assessed. They were asked to name and describe the tools represented by the icons. They were also asked to create a picture from a clear screen using the tools of their choice, write their name on the picture and print the finished picture. Throughout this process they were observed and their actions noted; help was only given at their request or when they made an error.

The following words are used to describe the results: 'nearly all' means over 90 per cent; 'most' means over 75 per cent; 'over half' means between 60 per cent and 75 per cent; 'half' means between 40 per cent and 60 per cent; 'less than half' means between 30 per cent and 40 per cent; 'some' means between 10 per cent and 30 per cent; and 'few' means less than 10 per cent (see Table 7.1).

The icons which are a pictorial representation of objects in the children's immediate experience of creating pictures were quickly recognised. For example, the majority of children identified the paintbrush and the shapes correctly and, associated these with their experience of art activities, enabling them to make a link with the function in the computer application. The spray can and roller of the Spray and Fill icons were recognized by some children, particularly those who had had the opportunity to handle and use these items. However, most of the children found it difficult to link these objects with functions in the application and describe the effects that would be achieved. For example, they were unable to associate painting a wall with a roller, with filling in a large space on the program, *Splosh*. The Text, Undo and Brush Size icons were not

Table 7.1 How pupils use icons (results for the full sample N=52)

Tool and function	Children's response	A	B	C	D
Brush: Main tool for painting or drawing lines on paper.	Visual recognition	46	3		3
	Visual recognition after one week	52			
	Recognition after practical exploration	52			
	Independent use during task	52			
Brush size: Changes size of current tool and shows current colour.	Visual recognition	4	10	16	22
	Visual recognition after one week	38		14	
	Recognition after practical exploration	33	9	10	
	Independent use during task	36			
Spray: Creates a dotted spray effect.	Visual recognition	7	9	20	16
	Visual recognition after one week	12	28	2	10
	Recognition after practical exploration	44	7	3	
	Independent use during task	45			
Fill Fills an enclosed area with colour.	Visual recognition	9	27	6	8
	Visual recognition after one week	28	18	6	
	Recognition after practical exploration	52			
	Independent use during task	16			
Circle/Triangle/Line: Enables shapes to be drawn.	Visual recognition	50			2
	Visual recognition after one week	52			
	Recognition after practical exploration	52			
	Independent use during task	15			
Text: Enables text to be painted onto the picture.	Visual recognition	6	16	30	
	Visual recognition after one week	22		30	
	Recognition after practical exploration	10		42	
	Independent use during task	36			
Undo: Cancels last mouse action.	Visual recognition	2	6	44	
	Visual recognition after one week	16	14		22
	Recognition after practical exploration	17	26	9	
	Independent use during task	20			
Colour bar/Palette: Colours available for use by brush/spray/fill tools	Visual recognition	52			
	Visual recognition after one week	52			
	Recognition after practical exploration	52			
	Independent use during task	52			

Notes: A = correct function described; B = icon described but not its function; C = function and icon not known; D = alternative suggestions made. We would like to acknowledge and thank Keyboard Technology, Kudlian Soft, Research Machines and Topologika Software for the use of their software in this study.

consistently recognised. The children who could read the text labels were able to make a more accurate or informed guess at the function, than those who could not. However, the abstract nature of the pictorial representation of the icon and the children's inability to make an association between this and something they recognised within their own experience seemed to prevent the children from recognising or suggesting a function for these icons. This is an important observation as it has implications for the way in which computer programs are introduced to pupils. An interesting task for a teacher is to try out a program that is new to them by trying to guess what all the icons mean before trying them out, asking someone else, or reading a manual.

Recognition of icons through practical exploration

Through exploration of the Brush and Colour Bar all of the children were able to describe the function of these icons and demonstrated this without further support. All of the children were able to describe the purpose of the Fill tool after they had used it, as a tool which 'fills in' a whole area but required further demonstration of the need for the area to be enclosed to fully understand its function. Most children correctly described the Spray tool after they had used it and used appropriate language to convey the action. Three children could not describe or could not discriminate between the Brush and the Spray. The more experienced children used the word 'spray' to describe the action.

All of the children identified the function of the Circle, Rectangle, Triangle and Line tools but many were unable to achieve making shapes unaided and needed demonstration to complete these independently. This appeared to make the children question whether they were right in their judgement and they were frustrated that they could not draw shapes more easily. This was particularly the case with the Triangle tool where the user is required to click on the three points of the triangle, before the shape is achieved. So, although the children believed these icons enabled the drawing of shapes, their practical experience of this did not really confirm or support this belief. Even with practical experience of the Undo icon, few children recognised its function. As the function is to only undo the last mouse action, where this was a small movement or mark on the screen, the children often did not see that the action had been undone. Even when they clicked on the icon for a second time, which reproduces the action, some children did not notice what had happened and could not identify the function. When the children clicked on the Text icon, only a small number noticed the insertion of the caret. Interestingly, two children recognised this as the same screen character as they had seen in a word-processing program and quickly realised that they could use the keyboard to insert text. A small number of children identified that clicking on the icon enabled writing and, with prompting, tested this by trying the keyboard. All of the children needed some prompting to fully explore the Brush Size tool. The children were told to click on the large and small arrows but needed to be prompted to explore the effect this had on the size of the tool they were using. Once this had been experienced, the children were able to fully explain the function of the arrows and the Brush Size icon. The children were then prompted to change the colour using the Colour Bar and then most of them recognised that the colour of the circle changed to match the colour they had selected.

The opportunity to explore the icons and then describe the function rapidly increased the children's understanding of some of the icons, particularly the Spray and Fill tools. Being able to see the effect achieved with these tools, the children found it easier to describe the function by pointing and demonstrating the effect. They were not so dependent on their language skills. The children who had been told the word 'spray' used it frequently to describe the effect of the Spray tool, but other children still conveyed the function effectively using language within their general vocabulary, for example 'it makes little dots'. All of the children were confident that they understood the function of the Brush and Colour Bar icons and demonstrated this independently, selecting colours and making brush strokes across the screen. Practical experience of these icons confirmed their understanding of the function from their visual recognition.

Measuring children's applied skills

The children tackled the task of creating their own picture with confidence and used some of the icons independently. They all used the Brush and the Colour Bar, but some were content to just use these two tools. These children were prompted to try to change the size of the brush and use other effects but could not remember or work out from the icons how to achieve this. Most children used the Brush Size tool to adjust the size of the Brush but some needed help to decrease the size using the small arrow. None of the children appeared to use the colour of the circle to check the colour selected, but preferred to look at the colour of the end of the paintbrush or the contents of the spray can. Most children used the Spray and selected the colour for this, but only a small number changed the size using the Brush Size tool. Some children used the Fill tool, while the remainder of the children filled in areas using the Brush tool. Some of the children tried to find colours which were not available on the Colour Bar.

Some children tried to use the Circle, Rectangle, Triangle and Line tools, but needed support to achieve the shape and to position it. All of the children made mistakes that they wished to erase, but only half of the children used the Undo function to achieve this. The other children recognised that they could over-paint an error or use white paint to 'rub out' a mistake and preferred to use this method.

Writing and then printing a picture

The children were asked to 'write' their name on the screen but a lot of them did not remember which icon to use to achieve this. All of the children needed help to complete this, either to position the caret in the correct place or prompting to change the colour in the Colour Bar so that they could see their text.

The final part of the task was to print the picture. The children were asked if they could find an icon or something on the screen which would achieve this. Most children located the printer icon on the icon bar and believed that clicking on this would print their picture. Two children who had previous experience of a word-processing package remembered that they needed to use the Menu button and then located the Print command. When asked to look at the keyboard, some children found the Print key and printed their picture in this way. The other children were all shown how to use the Menu button and asked to look for Print in the list of commands. Locating the method to print a picture was confusing for all the children and they all scanned the toolbar on *Splosh* for an icon which would achieve this. The children were creative and increased their search to the whole screen and most found the printer icon on the icon bar.

The children tackled their task with confidence and were content to work with some of the icons independently. All of the children were able to create a picture using the Brush and Colour Bar but some needed prompting to extend and develop their work. Most of the children had retained their recognition of the icons from their practical exploration and if they were prompted, for example, to increase their brush size they immediately pointed to the correct icon. Where the children had not fully recognised or understood a function and its icon, they were reluctant to try it and did not use it independently. The limited range of colours on the Colour Bar was frustrating for some children, as they could not locate some of the basic colours they wanted for their pictures.

Making mistakes and the use of 'Undo'

Most of the children at some stage wanted to 'undo' a mistake but were not really sure of how the Undo function worked. This function was also not effective for some of the 'mistakes' as it would only undo the last action, and some of the mistakes were made up of several mouse movements. However, all of the children were creative in solving this problem and found alternative methods of making the desired changes to their work. Several of the children chose to use white paint as a rubber and said this method 'worked better' than the Undo function. Undo is a concept associated with computing that is very different from other aspects of life – it is difficult to 'undo' many normal actions and especially ones related to real paint!

Most of the children avoided the shape tools and preferred to draw freehand because they were not confident using these tools. The major issues appeared to be controlling the size and the position of the shape, which often 'jumped' on top of the children's work and they then felt they could not remove it and that their picture was spoilt.

Importantly, some children transferred their experience of another application and using the mouse Menu button, experimented to see if the same result could be achieved in *Splosh*. Operating the Print button on the keyboard was effective for the children who found this and simpler than using the Menu button. A few children were concerned when the Menu window opened on top of their picture and needed reassurance that their picture would not be spoilt. Most of the children who used the Menu button were able to scan down the list of commands and effectively use their letter recognition skills to locate a word beginning with 'p'. Although the children achieved this with adult support, an icon with a picture of a printer located on the toolbar of *Splosh* would have made the operation simpler and enabled the children to achieve this independently.

Long-term visual recognition

A second assessment of the children's visual recognition of the icons was carried out one week later after the children had had substantial practical experience of using the painting program. There is an important aspect of ICT work called 'capability'. An ICT capable pupil is one that can, at a later stage, apply their knowledge and understanding to new situations. In our study there was a substantial increase in the results for some of the icons but not others. For example, on the initial assessment only four children identified the function of Brush Size, but on the second assessment most children described the function correctly. A similar increase was demonstrated by the Text, Fill and Undo functions. Only five more children recognised the Spray function on the second assessment which was surprising as nearly all of the children had used this tool extensively in their independent work. A possible explanation for this is that the majority of children found it hard to describe the effect of Spray and did not have the vocabulary to do this adequately. It is important that teachers record ICT performance in terms of 'can do' rather than 'did do' thus ensuring that the records reflect the pupils' capabilities.

The children were confident using the application, learnt rapidly and did not show any concerns about exploring the majority of icons. The assessment of the children's visual recognition of the icons was heavily dependent on the children's language and communication skills and, many of the children did not have the range of qualitative vocabulary to effectively describe the function of an icon.

It was observed that children responded quite differently to presentation of certain icons. The icons with a clear picture of an object, in the child's experience of art activities, were quickly identified by the children and the function linked to the object. The icons with a picture of an object in the child's experience but not generally associated with art activities, were identified but the function was not remembered. The children did not understand the metaphor of the spray can or roller and required practical experience of the function, in order to link the icon to the function. Recognition of these icons was not retained as readily over a period of one week, as those associated with art activities. There were two groups of children. Only one group was given experience of the physical objects associated with the tools and icons before meeting the computer program. That pre-experience included talking about painting a picture and the 'things' they would use to achieve this. Where children were given the opportunity to handle and experience objects, such as the spray can and roller, they were more able to associate the object and the pictorial representation of the icon with the function and developed a clearer understanding of the metaphor.

Although the icons were understood, this alone did not necessarily enable children to use them. ICT capability is more than giving children experience but enabling sustained and informed use of software interfaces over time. The research shows that pupils have the capacity to remember icons and function for a period of time, but the physical skill activity is not so easily remembered.

'Forgiveness' in the user interface

The children quickly learned a function and used it independently if it was simple, flexible and 'forgiving'. Although the shape tools were recognised by all of the children, they were not used by the majority in their independent work because the children did not fully understand how to use them, the skills required were more complex and the children found it hard to remove their mistakes. Functions that are forgiving are those that can be intuitively undone. Two unforgiving actions are printing and text entry. It was observed that some children tried to click on their text to change it (as they would with a word processor) but this simply created more inappropriate text.

Although some children recognised that the 'T' of the Text icon was associated with 'writing', none of the children knew the word 'text' to be able to make the link. The effect of selecting the Text icon would be more obvious to young children if the caret was contained in a frame or was bolder and blinking. The majority of children were unable to read 'Undo' on the Undo icon and, even where they could, they did not understand what this meant in relation to the application. As reported above, children did not use the Undo facility and apparently did not understand the concept. This is disappointing because the power of computer-based painting is the provisionality of the product. Hayes (2005) reported that slightly older children could use the Undo function with understanding and therefore it should be investigated whether this is an age related ability or whether the features of the icon or computer action (single Undo history) are the limiting factors. A more abstract symbol, such as a red X, may have been more effective in conveying that this could be used to remove mistakes. A sequence of Xs may indicate that several Undos are possible.

The colour palette should contain colours young children know and want to use in their work, for example, some palettes do not contain pink or brown; some of the children wanted to draw pictures of themselves. The Undo function is not sufficient for removing errors. A rubber or similar function would have enabled them to remove some mistakes more simply. Painting in white or the same colour as the background for example, is a difficult concept for some children to understand and a negative way of learning.

Summary of the main findings

Young children are able to use a simple graphical user interface independently and effectively. Young children learn rapidly and we should have high expectations of their skills and capacity to learn with computers. They are able to independently recognise and use the graphic symbolism of icon design and associate these with functions in an application, providing the representation on the icon is within the realm of their experience. Icons are more readily understood by the young child if he or she has direct experience of it and can associate it with the activity offered by the application. For example, young children associate a paintbrush with creating a picture but they do not generally associate a spray can or a roller. Where a function represented by an icon is more abstract, young children are able to learn the function through practical experience and retain it, providing it is easy to use and they are able to operate it independently. They do not need to understand the metaphors. However, there is a need for the standardization of metaphors and icons between programs. Young children are able to learn and operate abstract functions represented by metaphors, but this learning can be further facilitated and consolidated by a common approach between programs. Importantly, pupils are seen to develop their creativity and begin to express their ideas through the use of the computer. Although not documented, the use of the computer enables the children to express the conceptual ideas of creativity such as Colour, Brush type, Undo and Palette.

The effect of selecting an icon should be clear and immediate to the child, so that the effect of choice can be quickly seen. Direct manipulation and more subtle features are not always recognised by young children. Simpler effects, such as an icon changing colour on selection may be more effective. Animation of some icons may assist understanding of more abstract functions. It is important to be aware of whether the pupils see these subtleties, and to assist them in that process.

Wherever possible, verbal instructions should be avoided. The child becomes frustrated and loses independence if faced by a menu of written choices. Pictures and symbols should be used wherever possible. Young children are, however, able to learn a sequence of actions to achieve a function but need to be taught to do this.

Teachers have an immense understanding of the capabilities and skills of young children and they should be more involved in the design of educational software to ensure the applicability of icons to functions and that there is sufficient control over their appearance to meet the needs of the pupils.

Young children are confident to experiment and learn by trial and error. Software for young children needs to be flexible and forgiving to allow them to learn in this way. Error messages should be pictorial and easy to rectify. The organization of the screen should be simple and logical. The functions to Print, Save, Load and Exit should be icon-based and the process should be as simple as possible, that is, by restricting options and using pictures and symbols. The skills and interests of the child must be considered in the design, for example, the colours offered in the palette should be those recognised and wanted by young children and icons should be large enough not to require very precise mouse control.

Programs should allow customization by an adult to allow the child to learn progressively, gain confidence over a period of time and not be overwhelmed by too many choices. New functions can then be added as the child becomes more accomplished or requires additional options. There is a need to establish whether interface metaphors and language should be those within the experience of the young child or whether the young child should be taught specific computer language and concepts, as part of their computer-based learning experiences. The evaluation of usability was administered purely in terms of the interface icons and operating the software. There was little consideration of the implications of usability features for the use of the programs to achieve educational goals. This opens a different perspective for the evaluation of the usability of the software.

The implications for classroom practice are important and clear. Teachers and assistants should be:

- making informed decisions regarding the purchase of software;
- making explicit to the children the relationship between icon, name and function through a multiplicity of approaches;
- developing a child's visual literacy through the manipulation of images;
- ensuring that physical painting is promoted as a means of developing expression;
- developing a sense of enjoyment and satisfaction from success;
- exploiting the generalizations with other learning and developing those connections.

For many children, the painting program is the first experience of using the computer to be creative. Up until this point they would have used content programs such as adventure games, reading materials and interactive multimedia. In the main, those programs guide the user and give them limited and contextualised choices. The painting program, like word-processing and other generic programs, is different. The child starts with a blank screen and needs to make choices without any further prompt other than the icons presented. The research shows that learning is mediated by the computer itself, but pupils are dependent upon their own computer visual literacy and their capability is influenced by the teachers' contextualization of the activities.

The design of the painting interface is a metaphor based upon the palette and tool set. Its iconization is not standard across all programs and one major factor in its success in enabling children to use the program is the appropriateness of the pictorial representation. Teachers should be involved in the design of the software.

References

Dowling, M. (1995) *Starting School at Four: A Joint Endeavour*. London: Paul Chapman Publishing.

Evans, P. and Fuller, M. (1996) 'Hello. Who Am I Speaking To?' Communicating with pre-school children in educational research settings, *Early Years*, (autumn) 17(1).

Hayes, M. (2005) The children's voice. Unpublished PhD thesis, Lancaster University.

Jones, T. (1993) Recognition of animated icons by elementary-aged children, in *ALT-J*, 1(1): 40–6.

Lynch, P. (1994) Visual design for the user interface: Design fundamentals, *Journal of Biocommunications*, 21(1): 22–30.

Nourot, P. and Van Hoorn, J. (1991) Symbolic play in preschool and primary settings, *Young Children*, September.

Potter, G. (1996) From symbolic play to symbolic representation in early literacy: Clarifying the links, *Early Years*, 16(2).

Redmond-Pyle, D. and Moore, A. (1995) *Graphical User Interface Design and Evaluation (GUIDE): A Practical Process*. London: Prentice Hall.
Rosen, C. (1974) The effects of socio-dramatic play on problem-solving behaviour among culturally disadvantaged pre-school children, *Child Development*, 45(4): 920–7.
Vygotsky, L.S. (1978) *Mind in Society*. Cambridge, MA: Harvard University Press.

8
DIGITAL ANIMATION IN THE EARLY YEARS: ICT AND MEDIA EDUCATION

Jackie Marsh

This chapter focuses on the use of ICT in early years settings to facilitate the production of moving image texts – in this case, animated films. The chapter focuses in detail on a research project in which 3- and 4-year-old children in one nursery produced digital, animated films. The wide range of skills, knowledge and understanding developed in this activity is outlined and the implications of this work for policy and practice in early childhood education are discussed. This work took place as part of a broader emphasis on media education, which incorporates both film production *and* analysis, in this particular nursery. Initially, therefore, I will review the place of media education in the early years curriculum.

Media education

Media education in the UK has been confined primarily to the secondary phase of education. Indeed, it is often stated that media studies is one of the fastest growing subjects (Buckingham 2003), despite being derided in some quarters as an apparently easy option (Lee 1999). There has been very little work undertaken in primary years in relation to media education and there is even less evidence of its presence in the early years curriculum.

This is despite the growing prevalence of media texts in young children's lives. From birth, children are immersed in a media rich world (Rideout et al. 2003; Knobel 2005; Marsh 2005, 2006). There is evidence that preschool children are engaged in a range of complex practices outside of the nursery which includes accessing websites, using interactive games on digital and satellite television, playing with mobile phones and using games consoles, such as PlayStation (Marsh 2005). In the *Digital Beginnings* study (Marsh et al. 2005), for example, 1852 parents of children aged from birth to 6 in England were surveyed in order to identify how their children used popular culture, media and new technologies in the home. There was widespread evidence that children were immersed in digital practices from a very young age and, by the time they attended early years settings for the first time, many were already competent with a range of technologies. It would seem important, therefore, to enable them to develop further their critical skills in relation to media so that they become as skilful at navigating media texts as many appear to be in relation to print-based texts.

Media education involves a wide range of skills, knowledge and understanding, developed in relation to various media, such as moving image (film and television), the Internet, radio, newspapers and magazines. While all of these elements are important, it has often been the case that media production has been ignored at the expense of analysis (Buckingham 2003). However, there is little doubt that work on moving image production in particular develops a range of skills, knowledge and understanding (for an outline of some of these, see bfi 2003). Burn and Leach (2004), as part of a systematic review on the use of ICT in English, reviewed 12 studies in the UK which focused on moving image production. Of these 12 studies, four took place in primary schools; none were undertaken in nurseries. Burn and Leach suggested that moving image production was important because it drew on the knowledge that children develop in their everyday lives and it often involved collaborative work. In addition, the studies reviewed also suggested that work with moving image is highly motivational and, in some cases, can lead to increased attainment in print-based literacy (Parker 1999).

Reid et al. (2002) evaluated a project in which children in 50 schools worked on digital filming and editing. They suggested that the evidence from this project indicated that digital video production can:

- increase pupil engagement with the curriculum;
- promote and develop a range of learning styles;
- motivate and engage a wider range of pupils than traditional teaching methods, so providing greater access to the curriculum.

(Reid, et al. 2002: 3)

Because digital video production involves visual media, it can offer opportunities for those children who are more comfortable and competent with the visual mode to succeed. However, one of the main findings from this study was that teachers were often working with little knowledge of what they could expect from this kind of work. Because of a lack of curriculum guidance in this area, there is no developmental sequence which can be applied to children's work. This can lead to children repeating the same experiences in future years, or failing to address particular aspects of editing. In addition, some teachers have had little training in media production and so are not able to support children's learning effectively. In the projects reviewed by Reid et al. (2002), practice varied widely, from teachers who scaffolded tasks very well to teachers who simply gave cameras to pupils and let them get on with it. While there is now more guidance for early years and primary teachers (bfi 2003), there still needs to be more extensive focus on teachers' professional development in this field if media production is to take place in nurseries and primary schools. A further difficulty can be presented by the fact that the boundaries between different kinds of texts are very blurred and are becoming increasingly fluid in this digital world. This can lead to some confusion about what the nature of literacy is and how print-based literacy relates to work on media and moving image. There are key differences between modes and these differences need to be understood by teachers in work relating to media, otherwise confusions about the aims and outcomes of specific activities could arise. In addition, while there is evidence that work on moving image and media can have a positive effect on print-based literacy (PNS/UKLA 2005), it is important not to always use media to extend skills and understanding in relation to the alphabetic code, as this privileges the written word and means that insufficient focus is placed on skills and understanding in relation to media texts. Therefore, while the literacy curriculum should be revised to reflect the porosity of texts in the new media age, there still needs to be specific attention paid to media education if children are to develop appropriate knowledge and understanding.

The relationship between digital film production and ICT is, of necessity, close. Digital filming and editing requires the use of a wide range of ICT hardware and software, including various types of cameras (digital video, digital still, Digital Blue cameras, webcams, cameras on mobile phones); computers (desktops and laptops); editing software (e.g. Adobe Premiere, iMovie, Kartouche, Windows MovieMaker); or packages which combine a range of features, such as Lego Studio. In addition, some film production can involve the use of microphones and projectors to play back the films. There has been a perception in some quarters that young children are unable to operate complex hardware and software and that this precludes them from being involved in media production (Gauntlett 1996). However, as the chapters in this book attest, that position underestimates the knowledge and skills of young children and fails to recognise that as soon as a child is able to control a mouse or touch screen, they can begin to explore software in an independent manner.

This brief review of media education in relation to the early years has identified a significant gap in the knowledge base. We simply have very little knowledge about what young children might be able to do in this field. The rest of this chapter will outline a project in which 3- and 4-year-old children made digital, animated films. This project was undertaken in order to identify the range of skills, knowledge and understanding developed in this kind of work and to explore the implications for curriculum and professional development. While it is recognised that small-scale projects such as this will not be sufficient to inform curriculum change, they can offer glimpses into some of the opportunities and challenges faced by this kind of work. In the following section, I will provide a brief overview of the project itself.

The project

The study reported on in this chapter was undertaken in a nursery in the north of England over a period of one academic year. The nursery serves very diverse racial and linguistic communities, with a large number of refugee families located in the area. During the study, an 'animation studio' was set up in one corner of the nursery on a regular basis. This consisted of one or two laptops, connected to which were webcams. There were a variety of props to hand for the animation: toy figures, artefacts and scenery. Some children planned their stories first using a storyboard, although the majority preferred not to plan them at all. The children filmed the plastic figures using webcams and they used a piece of film editing software, *iMovie2*, to edit the animations. The children chose to undertake the activity over the course of the school year and 53, 3- and 4-year-old children in total produced films. This chapter focuses on the work of two children: Chloe and Jasim, who were both 4 years of age. Chloe was dual heritage African-Caribbean and English. Jasim was a boy of Pakistani heritage who spoke Punjabi as a first language and English as an additional language. Chloe and Jasim had access to computers at home, but neither of them had engaged in animation work before.

The outcomes

Over the academic year in which the project took place, observations enabled the skills, knowledge and understanding developed in this activity to be mapped out, as outlined in Table 8.1.

This is not intended to be an exhaustive list; a range of other skills were also developed, dependent upon context. Neither do I intend to suggest that all of the children who took part in this activity acquired all of these; attainment depended, as it always does, upon prior knowledge and

Table 8.1 Knowledge, skills and understanding developed in the animation activity

	Actions	Knowledge, skills and understanding (the ability to):
Technical skills	Controlling the mouse:	• Move cursor to desired space; • use left-hand button to select; • click and drag.
	Using camera software: Using *iMovie 2* software:	• Find appropriate button for taking photograph. • Use various functions appropriately (e.g. timeline, stop/replay buttons, adding sounds).
Visual skills	Framing shots:	• Position characters and artefacts appropriately; • use close-ups, mid-shots and long-shots.
Understanding of narrative	Creating stories:	• Create a story with a beginning, middle and end; • create a story with one or more characters; • create a setting.
Understanding of multimodality	Using different modes:	• Understand the affordances of different modes; • be aware of the differences in affordances of various modes; • understand the processes involved in transduction across modes.
Awareness of audience	Creating films which reflected interests of peers:	• Identify themes which will interest the audience (family, play, jungles); • identify props and soundtracks which will attract the audience.
Critical skills	Reflecting on product, making changes where necessary:	• Identify aspects of the work which needed changing (e.g. shots which included their own hands); • identify features which were particularly successful in meeting audience's needs and repeating these (e.g. sound effects).

Understanding of genre (animation)	Creating stop–motion animation:	• understand the principles of stop-motion animation (i.e. that a series of still images portraying small changes in movement can, when placed together, create illusion of larger movements); • understand the importance of principles such as continuity.

experience and ability, in addition to contextual considerations. Some children, for example, were only able to capture images using the webcam and were unwilling to persist in the activity further in order to complete their film. However, this was the case with very few children; the majority were very focused on the task in hand, often engaged in the activity for one to two hours, as they watched other children produce films before they made their own.

In relation to the first section of Table 8.1, 'Technical skills', the children acquired the ability to use a range of ICT hardware and software. The majority of children who had sufficient mouse control were able to operate the camera and then edit their movie independently, once they had been shown how to do this or had watched others do it. A number of the children were highly competent in relation to these skills and came to the activity with a great deal of prior experience and understanding. This may not be surprising if we consider the evidence from studies mentioned previously, which outline the technological encounters of children from a very young age (Rideout et al. 2003; Knobel 2005; Marsh 2005, 2006; Marsh et al. 2005).

The second section of Table 8.1 refers to 'Visual skills'. As reported by Reid et al. (2002), this digital animation work enabled children to demonstrate their ability in the visual mode, often a preferred mode for many children. In addition, the visual is becoming more salient in a society which is focused so closely on the screen and, as Kress argues, 'The current landscape of communication can be characterised by the metaphor of the move from *telling the world* to *showing the world*' (Kress 2003a: 137). It will become increasingly important for children to be able to read the visual and, therefore, projects such as this are central to such future developments. In addition, it is often through production of particular kinds of texts that one begins to understand those texts in a critical way, and so a focus on manipulation of visual images may enhance children's abilities to read the images they encounter in a more critical manner.

The third category in Table 8.1 focuses on an 'Understanding of narrative'. The children's understanding of narrative structure was also a feature of the work undertaken in this study. Children were given the opportunity to develop their story on a storyboard first if they so wished.

Storyboards are used in film production to map out the narrative frame-by-frame. As an example, this is Chloe's storyboard (Figure 8.1):

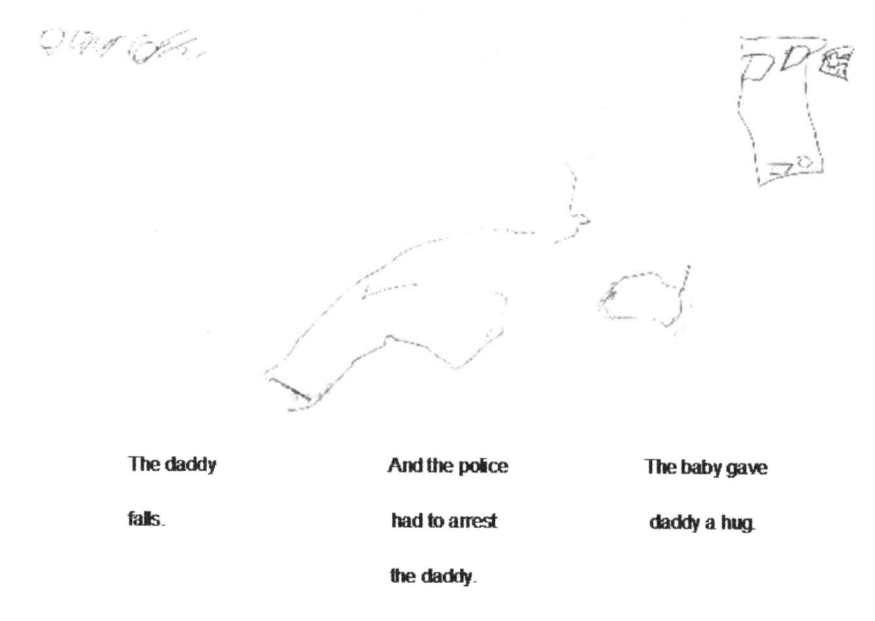

The daddy falls.

And the police had to arrest the daddy.

The baby gave daddy a hug.

Figure 8.1 Chloe's storyboard

This story demonstrates a grasp of narrative structure, as it features characters and a clear beginning, middle and end. Chloe followed her plan in the production of her film, as the stills illustrate (see Figure 8.2).

While her film includes more action than her storyboard, the key features of the narrative (Daddy getting arrested and the baby giving Daddy a hug) remained. From this activity, children developed an understanding of the nature of narrative structure, in that it is the same across different modes (different channels of communication). This was also the case with Mackey's (2002) study of older children, in which she found that they transferred understanding of narratives across media as they read a book, then played that story out in a computer game or watched it on film.

In relation to the fourth category in Table 8.1, 'Understanding of multi-modality' (communication using different modes), this was demonstrated in a wide range of ways. Here, I will focus on the interaction of the aural with the visual mode. Chloe, like many of the children, was very excited by the opportunity to add a soundtrack, which is easy to do in *iMovie 2* as all that is required is the dragging of an easily identifiable icon onto the timeline (on which the film clips are sequenced). There are a range of sounds to choose from in *iMovie 2* and Chloe went carefully through them all before choosing the sound of a whistling noise that sounded rather like

Figure 8.2 Stills from Chloe's film

a cartoon police siren. While this did not feature in her story on paper, Chloe had not been aware at that point of the existence of soundtracks. Once children were familiar with the soundtrack, they sometimes planned their stories to incorporate some of the sounds on *iMovie 2*. This work demonstrates that the children were developing an understanding of the *affordances* (Kress 2003b) of different media, that is, the kinds of things they allowed one to do and their particular properties. Because the digital film allowed sound, the children made the most of this opportunity and added sound to most of their films. In future digital animation, it would be useful, once children are confident about adding soundtracks, to develop their ability to identify when and what type of soundtrack would be most effective, rather than adding them indiscriminately as most children did in this project. However, it is important to remember that this was the children's first attempt at film production and so it was important to allow them to experiment with the soundtrack in this way. Some children re-told their story as a voice-over, using the in-built recording facility in *iMovie 2*. This, of course, was a practice familiar to them, with the extensive use of voice-overs in films and adverts. Indeed, it is tempting to think that children are becoming even more knowledgeable about film making processes in recent years because of the 'out-takes' features in many DVDs, which often show scenes on set, or discarded clips and retakes. Certainly, this film production work appeared to draw on the children's 'funds of knowledge' (Moll et al. 1992) developed in their out-of-school lives, in various ways. Many had an implicit understanding of aspects such as camera angle, lighting and setting. It is the role of educators to draw on this implicit knowledge and make it explicit, giving children the language needed to articulate their plans and actions in meaningful ways.

The fifth category, 'Awareness of audience', was an interesting process to observe. Dyson (1997, 2002) has emphasised the social nature of young children's writing in the classroom, in that they often write to entertain, impress, include or exclude others from social groups. A similar process occurred in relation to digital authorship. Boys in particular appeared to want to appeal to their audience's (boys') perceived interests. Many of their films featured the plastic jungle animals from the nursery's stock and these generally took part in a range of exciting and dangerous adventures which involved a lot of fighting and roaring. Indeed, Jasim and his friend Tahir decided to use a snatch of the *Jungle Book* soundtrack they had heard being played by a group of other boys as the soundtrack for a film they had produced based on a story about jungle animals. Of course, this was an instant hit with their peers. Girls were less inclined to pander to their audience's interests in these ways but, nonetheless, took care to develop stories which included characters they and their female peers were interested in, such as mothers, babies and princesses – a phenomenon witnessed in relation to written stories (Millard 2003). It is, therefore, of interest that this understanding of audience should transfer across modes in this way. The children were also aware of the animated films they and their peers had watched and enjoyed, such as *Finding Nemo, Toy Story 2* and *Shrek 2*, the characters or storylines from these films sometimes appeared in their films. Dyson (1999) notes that this appropriation of media material by children occurs not only in relation to content but also to the genres, graphic conventions (symbols and signs), voiced utterances (e.g. catch phrases) and ideologies of media texts (Dyson 1999: 378–80). In this study, this wide range of types of 'textual poaching' (Dyson 1999) was not apparent, but that may have been because the children were restricted to using props that consisted of plastic characters and animals which could not always be correlated to popular films. There is evidence from studies with older children (Reid et al. 2002) that they do incorporate popular culture into their moving image productions in numerous ways.

The penultimate category in Table 8.1, 'Critical skills', could be traced throughout the project. Many children were able to make critical judgements based on their understandings of the purpose and audience. For example, one child made a film which included her hand shown placing one of the characters. She noticed and commented on this and was careful not to repeat this in the second film she made. Another child noticed that his film contained images out of sequence, as he had not placed them in an appropriate order when editing. Indeed, it could be argued that the children's critical skills in relation to moving image texts were more developed than those in relation to print-based texts, because of their more extensive experience with moving image texts in the home.

The final category in Table 8.1, 'Understanding of genre', was the most challenging one for the children in this study. The genre in this particular case was animation. In animated films, still images are sequenced to portray movement and this can present a difficulty in terms of children's understanding of time and space in multimodal texts. For most children in this study, the three-dimensional sequencing of actions in a chronological narrative proved to be difficult (see Marsh (in press) for further discussion of this aspect of the study). Nevertheless, from the overall work in the project, it is clear that there are a number of learning opportunities offered in the development of animated films in the early years.

Once the sequence of skills, knowledge and understanding developed in the animation activity had been mapped out, it was easier for practitioners to identify the kinds of support that children needed in order to develop their skills. The next stage would be to develop this framework into a sequence of curriculum activities in order to inform further teaching and assessment. Such a sequence would indicate the stages children needed to go through in order to succeed in media production work, whilst acknowledging that linear progression through a sequence of stages is a problematic concept. Nevertheless, practitioners do need to be clear about the kinds of experiences children need in early stages of moving image media production in order to understand how to build on this effectively. In this activity, for example, it was clear that children needed to develop sufficient mouse control before being able to use the editing software. Table 8.1 provides a start to this kind of work as it outlines the kinds of learning which have taken place in this project and provides a map for future digital animation production.

Film production in the early years

This chapter has focused on one specific aspect of media education, that of animation production. However, there are many other areas of moving image production that could and are developed in early years settings. Live action filming, which involves children filming events and activities undertaken in daily life, either staged or impromptu, can also develop some of the skills, knowledge and understanding outlined in Table 8.1, as well as extend additional areas of knowledge. In this chapter, the emphasis has been on the production of narrative films, but it is important that children also have plenty of opportunities to produce non-narrative films. For example, children could choose favourite poems, paintings or pieces of music and make films that portray aspects of, and reactions to, those texts. In the nursery featured above, children have made films of their favourite aspects of nursery in order to inform new children of the range of activities that could be undertaken. It was interesting that many children chose to film outdoor activities, signalling that this was a significant feature of the provision for them. In addition, children should have an opportunity to share their work with a wider audience. Films can be re played using a projector and screen, or interactive whiteboard, which can enable group reflection and discussion. Finally, it is important to involve parents, carers and wider family members in this process. Saving children's work onto CD-ROM can enable parents to view films at home or in a community venue such as a public library. Just as many proud parents like to display their children's work on fridge doors and noticeboards, some may wish to celebrate their children's multimodal productions by viewing them on appropriate hardware. For parents who may not have access to relevant technology, film shows in settings featuring their children's work, to which they are invited, would be an important element to embed in this work.

Conclusion

In this chapter I have outlined a project in which aspects of moving image education were introduced into the curriculum of one nursery. This work indicates that very young children are able to develop digital, animated films if they are given appropriate resources and support. The range of skills, knowledge and understanding developed in this activity was very broad, and this project was only the beginning of this work for these children. It would be important in future years for them to extend these skills further, rather than endlessly repeating some of these activities or, worse, not returning to them at all. For this to happen, however, there would need to be a concerted effort by policy makers to develop a meaningful framework for media education in the foundation and primary stages. There may be currently an opportunity for this to happen at some level, with the government's recent emphasis on 'media literacy'. This term now has wide currency within the UK as a result of the Office for Communication's (Ofcom) remit to develop media literacy among the general population. Ofcom define media literacy as 'the ability to access, understand and create communications in a variety of contexts' (Ofcom 2004). If children are going to be able to 'create communications in a variety of contexts', then they need opportunities to do so, opportuntities which are embedded in a rigorous and comprehensive framework. This might then provide teachers with the kind of support they need if digital media production is to be taken seriously in schools. If this does not happen, then many teachers may continue to feel dazzled by the speed of technological changes taking place and unable to provide curriculum content which is appropriate for a digital generation (Luke and Luke 2001). Given the proliferation of digital communication in recent years, and popular phenomena such as blogging (the creation of online web diaries), moblogging (the updating of online blogs visually and textually through authors' mobile phones) and shared databases of photographs which form the basis for group discussion (see Flickr at www.flickr.com), this generation of children are going to need to be digitally adept if they are going to be able to participate in these particular 'communities of practice' (Lave and Wenger 1991). Of course, such skills are not just important for social purposes, there are also economic and political implications for the future workforce. The kinds of skills and knowledge demonstrated by the children in this study, and their ability to move across modes and media with ease, are going to be vitally important in the years ahead. Given this, the question with regard to the place of media education (or 'media literacy') in the early years is an urgent one; we ignore it at our peril.

References

bfi (British Film Institute) (2003) *Look Again: A Teaching Guide to using Film and Television with Three- to Eleven-Year Olds*. London: BFI Education.

Buckingham, D. (2003) *Media Education: Literacy, Learning and Contemporary Culture*. Oxford: Polity Press.

Burn, A. and Leach, J. (2004) ICTs and moving image literacy in English, in R. Andrews (ed.) *The Impact of ICTs on English 5–16*. London: RoutledgeFalmer.

Dyson, A.H. (1997) *Writing Superheroes: Contemporary Childhood, Popular Culture, and Classroom Literacy*. New York: Teachers College Press.

Dyson, A.H. (1999) Coach Bombay's kids learn to write: Children's appropriation of media material for school literacy, *Research in the Teaching of English*, 33: 367–402.

Dyson, A.H. (2002) *Brothers and Sisters Learn to Write: Popular Literacies in Childhood and School Cultures*. New York: Teachers College Press.

Gauntlett, D. (1996) *Media, Gender and Identity: An Introduction*. London: Routledge.

Knobel, M. (2005) *Technokids, Koala Trouble* and *Pokémon*: Literacy, new technologies and popular culture in children's everyday lives, in J. Marsh and E. Millard (eds) *Popular Literacies, Childhood and Schooling*. London: RoutledgeFalmer.

Kress, G. (2003a) Interpretation or Design: From the world told to the world shown.

In M. Styles and E. Bearne (eds) *Art, Narrative and Childhood*. Stoke-on-Trent: Trentham.

Kress, G. (2003b) *Literacy in the New Media Age*. London: Routledge.

Lankshear, C. and Knobel, M. (2004) Text-related roles of the digitally 'at home'. Paper presented at the American Education Research Association Annual Meeting, San Diego, 15 April.

Lave, J. and Wenger, E. (1991) *Situated Learning*. Cambridge: Cambridge University Press.

Lee, C. (1999) War exposes futility of media degrees, *Times Educational Supplement*, 7 May.

Luke, A. and Luke, C. (2001) Adolescence lost/childhood regained: On early intervention and the emergence of the techno-subject, *Journal of Early Childhood Literacy*, 1(1): 91–120.

Mackey, M. (2002) *Literacies Across Media: Playing the Text*. London: RoutledgeFalmer.

Marsh, J. (ed.) (2005) *Popular Culture, New Media and Digital Technology in Early Childhood*. London: RoutledgeFalmer.

Marsh, J. (2006) Global, local/public, private: Young children's engagement in digital literacy practices in the home, in J. Rowsell and K. Pahl (eds) *Travel Notes from the New Literacy Studies: Case Studies in Practice*. Clevedon: Multilingual Matters.

Marsh, J. (in press) Emergent media literacy: Digital animation in early childhood, *Language and Education*.

Marsh, J., Brooks, G., Hughes, J., Ritchie, L., Roberts, S. and Wright, K. (2005) *Digital Beginnings: Young Children's Use of Popular Culture, Media and New Technologies*. Sheffield: University of Sheffield. Available at: http://www.digitalbeginnings.shef.ac.uk/

Millard, E. (2003) Gender and early childhood literacy, in N. Hall, J. Larson and J. Marsh (eds) *Handbook of Early Childhood Literacy*. London: Sage.

Moll, L., Amanti, C., Neff, D. and Gonzalez, N. (1992) Funds of knowledge for teaching: Using a qualitative approach to connect homes and classrooms, *Theory into Practice*, 31(2): 132–41.

Ofcom (2004) *Ofcom's Strategies and Priorities for the Promotion of Media Literacy: A Statement*. Available at: http://www.ofcom.org.uk/consult/condocs/strategymedialit/ml_statement/strat_prior_statement.pdf, March 2005.

Parker, D. (1999) 'You've read the book, now make the film': Moving image media, print literacy and narrative, *English in Education*, 33(1): 24–35.

PNS/UKLA (Primary National Strategy/United Kingdom Literacy Association) (2005) *Raising Boys' Achievement in Writing*. London: HMSO.

Reid, M., Burn, A. and Parker, D. (2002) *Evaluation Report of the BECTA Digital Video Pilot Project*. London: British Film Institute.

Rideout, V.J., Vandewater, E.A. and Wartella, E.A. (2003) *Zero to Six: Electronic Media in the Lives of Infants, Toddlers and Preschoolers*. Washington: Kaiser Foundation.

Robinson, M. (1997) *Children Reading Print and Television*. London: Falmer Press.

9

USING ICT TO ENHANCE THE LEARNING OF MUSIC

Mary Hayes, Chris Taylor and David Wheway

Everyone loves and enjoys music in their lives. Not all children will become professional musicians, but we need to teach them as though they might be one day. That way, they would have the sort of start that would make it possible for them to become musicians. This chapter addresses how teachers can help children to develop musically with the help of ICT. In the 1920s there were significant technological developments, with the invention of the gramophone and radio. The outcome of the introduction of those items into our culture was wider access to a great range of different types of music, but a loss of the aural memory tradition in music. These are issues that are addressed in the first part of the chapter.

The second part of this chapter offers a background to music technology. In terms of professional music making, the technology is changing continually with new items rapidly becoming obsolete and at the same time, old systems coming back into fashion. This technology has a great impact on the child's listening, and so it is useful for the teacher to know how the technology has shaped commercial music. While it may not seem directly necessary for teaching music in an early years' setting, it is important to be aware of a broader view of its development and the chapter provides technical advice.

Recording of sound was first invented around the start of the century with the phonograph. This used a cylinder to record sounds, initially covered with metal foil and subsequently wax. The sounds produced by machines were of low quality, and a high sound volume was required to create an impression on the cylinder. It was superseded by the 78 rpm record, which enabled copies to be made easily, and individual sections could be selected by placing the needle on the correct area of the disc. This invention has radically changed the development, marketing and performance of music. With the invention of the electronic valve, amplification of sound became possible. In the 1920s the first true electronic instrument called the 'Ondes Martenot' was invented. The electric guitar was introduced in the 1930s. This was initially of great importance in popular music as it allowed the guitarist to be heard behind the brass section of a dance band. By the 1940s, composers and technicians were experimenting with electronic instruments based on oscillators, which created sounds electronically, such as the Theremin. These offered new sounds to the composer's palette. All these innovations depended on the invention of electronic amplification and microphones to render the electronic waves into audible sounds. The invention of magnetic tape recording, shortly before World War II, let composers and experimenters of the late 1940s and 1950s experiment with tape-based effects, including changing speeds, repeating loops, artificial echo and reversal of sounds. The invention of electronic record players led to an improvement of the quality and volume of sound available in the home.

The electric organ was initially devised in the 1930s as a replacement for the Church pipe organ. This instrument offered another range of sounds accessible by any keyboard player. By the early 1960s it had become a mainstream instrument, being used in pop, jazz and 'easy listening' as well as for religious purposes. By the end of the 1960s use of electronics had really taken off. Multitrack recording enabled one person to build up a whole orchestra of sound. Sampled sounds from instruments such as the 'Mellotrons' offered the studio musicians a chance to simulate an orchestra or a choir through a keyboard. The invention of the 'Moog Synthesiser' enabled musicians to create, manipulate and process sounds in a wide variety of new ways. The width of one's imagination was the limit of the sound palette available to the musician. At the same time, groups such as *The Beatles* showed that it was not necessary to be a trained, literate musician to be an effective composer who could communicate with a wide audience.

Nowadays, a musician will be familiar with the use of digital (computer-based) and tape recording, a range of electronic instruments as well as acoustic ones. Many will have the ability to edit recorded music in the same way that text can be edited on a word processor, and to mix, enhance and reorganise sounds so that the final effect can be note perfect. In terms of the processing of sounds, it is possible to synthesise sounds (i.e. make and mix new sounds), to sample sounds (record any sound to play from a keyboard), to sequence sounds (to compose and record digitally, and then to edit the composition) and these technologies are used throughout classical, pop and jazz traditions.

These inventions have had an enormous impact upon our perceptions of music. We now expect to be able to listen to music, via the radio, TV or CD player, of a quality that would be impossible to reproduce in the concert hall. The inventions have changed society's perceptions of what music is, who plays it and where it can be heard.

In the sphere of music teaching, when these inventions began to be available for popular use, more emphasis began to be put on musical 'appreciation' (Borland 1927). Since then, arguments have developed to suggest that music needs to be taught differently, in order to ensure that professional musicians are able to understand music through aural means before beginning to learn notation (Kendell 1977; Paynter 1982). Odam (1995) later considered evidence that the right hemisphere of the brain deals with musical sound, intuition and holistic thought, while the left hemisphere is connected with linguistics and logic. Odam argued for musicians to be trained using aural memory before moving on to study notation, using a parallel with speaking and reading (1995: 33). He further argued that a strong musical experience should be built of complex patterns of sound before progressing with notation (1995: 47). Playing and learning through written symbols seems to be only a western tradition. It is not so in folk, jazz and other cultures, and African music is strongly related to vocal sounds – drumming follows the lines of tonal languages (Wiggins 1993: 24). Other cultures pass on music aurally and notation is often used *after* a creative act as a reminder of what the musician did. Van der Meer (1980: 139), when studying in India, found that it was quicker to learn the music first, than to make a notation. He also commented that Indian musicians trained first as vocalists. There is a short tradition in early years education of learning songs using names for the pitch of a scale linked to hand signals. It was developed in 1840 by Miss Glover as a system of notation (Rainbow 1967: 115) – this was a form of 'tonic solfa' later used by Kodaly (Taylor 1979: 49).

So how can ICT help to improve aural memory and develop musical experience? The chapter is structured around four aspects of developing a musical education that can be enhanced by using ICT. Those are:

1 Awareness of the children's sound environment: taking time to listen to and describe sounds from their environment, such as sounds from outside, on a trip, made from objects within their setting, hidden sounds, and of course music around them.
2 Responding to sound, showing an awareness of different ways of moving, at different speeds, and using these movements to respond to live or recorded music.
3 Categorizing sound by associating sounds with objects, moods, events,

when they are made (a woodblock sounding like knocking on the door, rubbing tambour skin like grass, tootling on a penny-whistle – a happy sound).
4 Recording, playing and changing sounds. Patterning with sound by putting two or more sounds or movements together, and recording the patterns.

Awareness of the sound environment

Sound is all around children, before birth as well as after. Deaf children respond to vibration and movement. Many parents influence their baby's mood through song. They use a special 'singing' voice when talking to the infant, while making eye contact. They buy recordings of songs, books with sounds, little keyboards and toy percussion as presents. They provide access to 'live' and recorded music – typically using TV programmes, DVDs, audio tapes and CDs. Music sets a mood. A library of CDs or tapes including stories, musical pieces, stories with music and interesting sounds to fit with a given theme is a good resource. Adults can help young children to record and then listen to sounds or simple compositions. They can listen to sounds recorded from the environment, discuss them in musical terms and even find simple drawings to represent the sounds – which could be used as starting points for sound compositions.

Many early years settings encourage use of the voice through singing. The voice is the one musical instrument available to practically all children. However, going beyond the reproduction of songs, by exploring the voice to discover mouth shapes, vocal quality (quiet/loud, whispering, happy imitation, etc.) has strong links with good vocal development and with language development.

Tait and Haach (1984: 34) argued that the development of imagery is an important step in a child's aesthetic education. They argued that aesthetic properties can be defined as patterns that emerge from the relationship of musical *elements and forms*. Teachers can help to develop an understanding of imagery by asking children about the sounds they hear and using a wide range of words to describe the sounds. Tait and Haach suggested that tones with higher partials (harmonics or overtones), result in what we call a 'bright' quality of sound, while tones with more and stronger lower partials may create the impression of a 'dark' quality (1984: 26). So it is helpful to the child to talk about and look at images when they listen to music. A computer enables the teacher to play a CD while presenting images on screen. The teacher can talk to the children about how the sounds make them feel, asking if it reminds them of experiences they have had at home or on holiday. The teacher can then help the children to increase their vocabulary.

Responding to sound

Parents play rhythmically with their children – jogging, swinging, bouncing and dancing. As children grow parents engage them in rhythmic walking rhymes and stair climbing songs. They swing their children between them as they walk. They share their children's growing fascination with the sound of feet walking through gravel, rainfall on the car roof, the sound of a saucepan tapped with a wooden spoon or a made-up song when out shopping.

In addition to being encouraged to describe the sounds and moods they experience, children need to become aware of sounds in space and time. This is what is beginning to happen when they move in response to the sounds they hear. Tait and Haach (1984: 37) claim that this is experiencing music in a metaphoric way. This means that it is removed from actual things, places or people, and is about the qualities of feeling and movement. Meadows (1993: 75) tells us that a metaphor helps us to 'express ideas that we lack the language to describe', it communicates in a 'compact manner', and by using it we can draw from one field of study to facilitate comprehension in another.

Teachers can help children to understand the quality of music by encouraging them to move and feel the music they hear, also through asking the children about the experience, widening their vocabulary and helping them to hear the 'character' of the music. They can create a sound track to go with visual presentations that includes a wide range of words from the computer thesaurus, or introduce spoken word and sound poems to the children. They can create or help the children to create image stores that children can recognise as having the same 'character' as the music it represents. The image however, needs to have a relationship with the music it represents *for the child*, not just for the teacher. Odam (1995) maintained that musical thinking and experience draws upon both metaphor and rational analysis. Musicians need to be able to synthesise both.

Categorizing and associating sounds

Scarfe (1977) was interested to know what the children themselves perceived when they listened to music. She worked with 4- to 5-year-olds and found that although they had great problems differentiating extremes of pitch, they could recognise the rise and fall of series of sounds. The children she worked with were responsive to images – such as flying high or crawling low, and used the metaphoric language of light, bright, friendly – or dark, fierce, angry. The children found the words 'heavy' and 'light' confusing at first in relation to music. Her research showed a musical equivalent to Bruner's research with Anglin (Bruner and Anglin 1973) about the child's representation of the world. She posited the following stages:

- Enactive – moving to the music, associating the music with images and metaphors.
- Iconic – seeing a picture of the image they described in the enactive stage and relating to it.
- Symbolic – children creating a notation of some kind that acts as a trigger back to the iconic stage.

As can be seen, the children provide their own description, image and notation. But Scarfe (1977) argues for aural experiences *first* in helping children to categorise and associate sounds.

Scarfe used a computer program that used graphic notation to have sound phrases linked to pictures. The children could listen and respond to sound phrases, compose music without 'notation', and the program made it 'impossible for the children to fail' (Pierson 1988: 1). In this way the children could generate complex patterns of sound and 'play' instruments. Pierson created the program so that 'the computer can perform the technical aspects of notation and performing, leaving the user free to explore' (1987: 26).

Recording, playing and changing sounds

Computer programs fall into two main categories. The first category is that of programs specifically written for educational use. The other category is programs that are free – either already on your computer or from the Internet. Within this second category there are a burgeoning number of school sites offering their own support materials and/or links to useful sites.

Types of programs include recording and playback, samplers, sequencers, loop-based programs, rhythm machines, synthesisers, composition tools, factual/research programs, song or vocal programs, virtual instruments and music concept training programs.

Not all programs are good, and many seek to provide an experience for the child that would be much better achieved away from the computer. Some seek to teach high-level skills by rote – and these can discourage rather than support learning.

Sequencing

There are a number of simple sequencing programs on the market, which are suitable for use with young children, and can engage them in useful musical learning if appropriately organised. Most use pictures of instruments (see Figure 9.1) or characters with linked sounds or phrases, which can be ordered into simple patterns, or 'sequences'. The sequences can usually be recorded and saved.

There are obvious links to both the broader curriculum and their own extended composition sequences. Sequencing programs such as these often offer the opportunity to change sounds, speed and dynamics – and these concepts can then be applied in other music activities. Here technology might be utilised as a precursor to the children's simple patterning of acoustic sounds, for instance on percussion. Current examples of such programs include, *Compose Junior*, *Black Cat Compose* and *2Explore* in Music Toolkit (see Figure 9.1).

Loop-based programmes

Loop-based programs offer short musical phrases which can be drawn or pasted onto tracks within the programs. A track is a musical line or row – and often programs will have a number of tracks which can play at the same time. Current examples include *Compose World Junior* where musical phrases can be put into a simple sequence and *Super-Duper-Music-Looper* (see Figure 9.2) where children select a variety of sounds and rhythms then draw or paint the sounds in each track. Such programs allow very fast creation of something more like music from a dance club than a classroom.

Rhythm machines

Many programs come with simple grids which can be filled to create rhythm layers. They are filled by clicking in the cells of the grids or dragging percussion sounds into cells. *2Simple* Music Software has a program called *2Beat*, which is fine for older children with adult support,

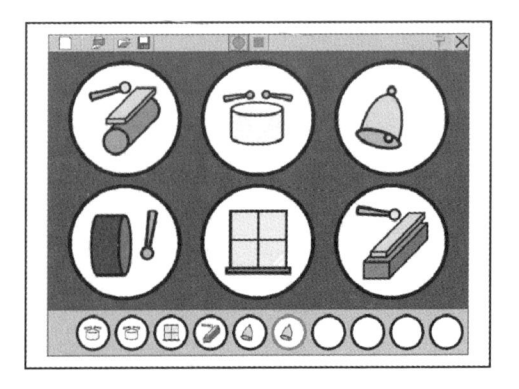

Figure 9.1 Sequencing illustration

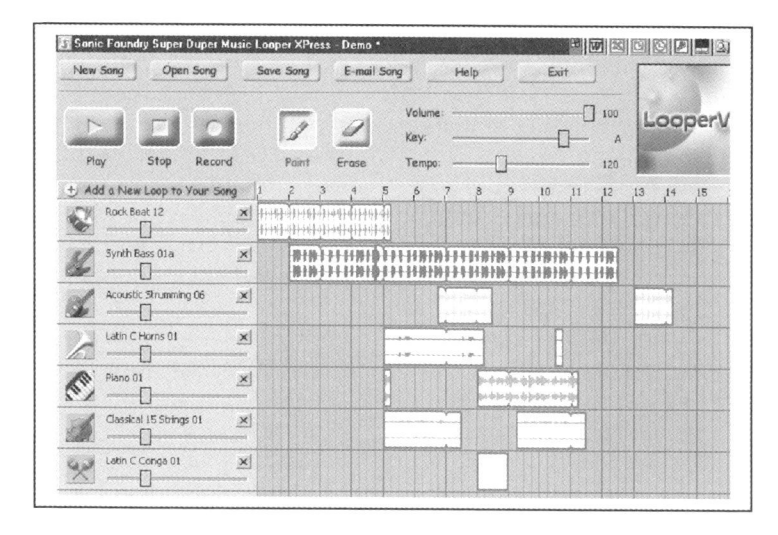

Figure 9.2 *Super Duper Music Looper*

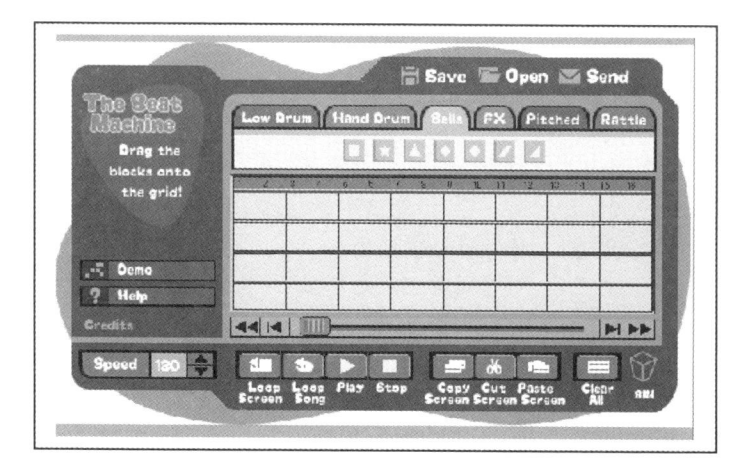

Figure 9.3 *The Beat Machine* from Radio 3s *Making tracks* website

as it is a free rhythm machine on Radio 3s website for children, *Making Tracks* at: http://www.bbc.co.uk/radio3/makingtracks/beatmachine.shtml (see Figure 9.3).

Types of technology available for music in early years settings

It is not suggested that all the musical possibilities posed are used in schools, rather that the teacher finds what is readily available and puts that to good purpose. It must be realised that in the field of music some specialist tools may be required, such as a microphone, amplifier and cassette recorder.

Owing to the increasing availability of computers in education it would seem sensible to emphasise their use in music. Other music technologies available might include audio tape recorders, microphones, CD players, keyboards and dance mats. Someone may have held on to older equipment (record players, reel-to-reel tape recorders, keyboards with samplers). Other technologies include minidisk recorders, MP3 recorders, amplifiers and speakers.

At first the technology can be overwhelming; however, in a short time, using the equipment becomes as much second nature as selecting TV channels or scanning for a radio station. The following section is intended to clarify some of the basics.

Microphones

The 'job' of a microphone depends on what the microphone is attached to. For the purpose of music technology, we should think of a microphone as something which captures sound – albeit very briefly. By attaching the microphone to different equipment we can do things with the captured sound – such as amplify, record or change the sound. Lots of equipment can use a microphone – so it is an extremely useful item to have. Computers often come with microphones and audio tape recorders sometimes have them attached. Karaoke machines have microphones as standard. You may have a PA (personal address) system or hi-fi used for fêtes and open days, which has a microphone.

Generally speaking – any microphone will do. Even earphones plugged into the 'sound-in' socket on equipment will work as a microphone! However, microphone cables can end in a variety of plugs including 'XLR', 'jack' or 'mini jack' (see Figure 9.4) If there is nowhere to plug in your microphone you'll require an adapter. The most common adapter for a computer to take a microphone is a large to mini jack adapter. These are widely available (electricity shops, computer sales) and cost a very small amount.

Recorders

A recorder allows the sound captured by the microphone to be stored and played back. The most common recorder for the past 30 years has been the audio cassette recorder. However, the quality of the recording and the frustration of searching for the start of a recording meant that other recording equipment superseded the cassette recorder. Some are portable (MP3, minidisk, DAT tape) – and some less so (computer, CD recorder, studio recording equipment). These other types of equipment not only offer

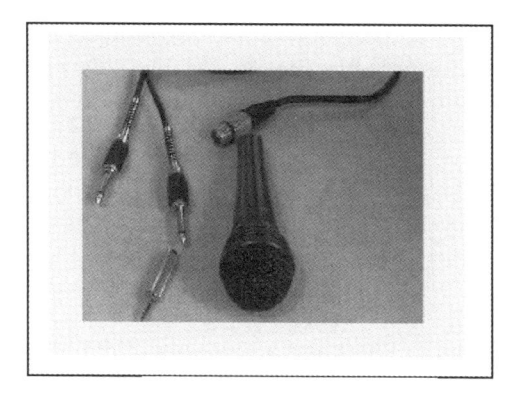

Figure 9.4 Cables from left: large jack, large jack with large to mini jack converter XLR

much higher quality recording, but once mastered, are much quicker to navigate. Most use standard icons for 'stop', 'play' 'fast-forward', etc. that can be found on household equipment such as the TV/video remote control (see Figure 9.5).

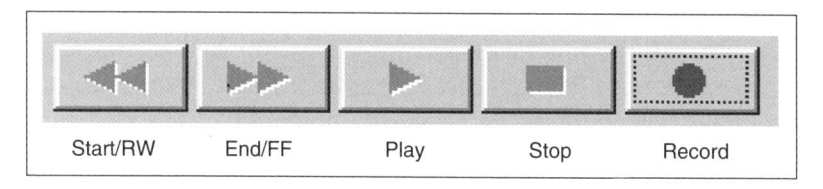

Figure 9.5 Standard icons on household recording equipment

Amplifiers

Most sound equipment has an amplifier. An amplifier is used to boost the sound – to make it louder and clearer or, of course, quieter. Within the home, items with amplifiers include telephones, answering machines, TVs, radios, electronic doorbells, computers, alarms, Hi-fi, audio tape recorders, karaoke machines and games machines. An amplifier is worth using to produce good quality sounds. Some loudspeakers come with their own amplifiers. These are known as 'powered speakers' (see later). With interactive whiteboard systems it is likely that there is an amplifier and speakers. You can use amplifiers in conjunction with keyboards, computers, minidisk and MP3 recorders and some audio cassette recorders.

Speakers

Also called 'loudspeakers'. Once sound has been amplified it needs to get out so it can be heard. Speaker cones within the speakers mirror the internal shape of our ears. This was more obvious when record players had large horn shaped trumpets attached to the stylus. Nowadays the cones are hidden behind a hard or soft mesh at the front of the speakers. Internal speakers in most equipment, such as tape recorders, CD players, keyboards and computers, produce relatively poor quality sound. Most equipment will have sockets for leads to be attached to external amplifiers and/or speakers, which can greatly enhance the quality and volume of the sounds being played or listened to.

Powered speakers

If the computer has speakers attached with leads, these will be powered speakers. Powered speakers have integral amplifiers so that the sound is amplified and released from the same source. If you have powered speakers there is often no need for an amplifier. However, many computer speakers are not suitably powered for use in large spaces such as classrooms.

Headphones

Headphones are useful if the sounds children are producing or listening to do not need to be heard by others. However, this means that there is little control over the volume of the sound and this has serious health and safety implications. Especially if children can increase the volume of the sound themselves, as they are unaware of the risks involved.

Audio recording

Some equipment can record and playback sounds which are collected via a microphone. These commonly include audio tape recorders, computers, microphones with in-built recorders, minidisk and MP3 recorders. Some electronic keyboards can also record and playback audio. The computer is one of the best recording devices available, it requires a soundcard (see soundcards), but most computers in educational establishments have these as standard. If you do need to purchase a soundcard expect to pay around £30 and, unless you are technically minded, arrange for a technician to fit the card.

Soundcards

These are hardware units attached to computers to enable sounds. They are essential if you wish to use your computer for music activities. There are three ways of finding out if the computer has a soundcard:

1 Look for a loudspeaker icon at the bottom right of you screen when you switch on.

2 If you hear a melody when you switch on your computer (once loaded) that means you have a soundcard.
3 Look at the back of your computer (or edge of a laptop). You should see something like Figure 9.6 with at least two sockets.

Most computers and laptops now come with at least basic soundcards.

Operations

Direct sound processing

This involves changing the nature of a sound instantly by use of some form of electronic or mechanical processing. A simple process is making sounds louder – or what is called amplification. Most settings have access to some form of amplification system. A child might talk or sing into a microphone connected to the amplifier. The amplifier then processes the sound by making it louder. Many children have never heard the sound of their own voice; an amplifier enables them to do this. Increasing or reducing the treble or bass can filter the sound, and effects can be added where available, such as echo or reverberation. In Figure 9.6, the microphone socket is illustrated with a microphone icon. On some soundcards and other machines you may see the abbreviation 'mic'.

Children may be familiar with systems used in home karaoke machines, where they can sing along to a backing tape. A further development of this is the microphone with a sound processor built in. These typically include preset voice effects, applause, laughter and drum sounds. Such equipment is usually marketed for the home entertainment market, but it gives children the opportunity to see how sounds can be changed electronically. It also has the advantage of being relatively cheap. Uses might be to add sound effects to an assembly or a play.

Shy children who lack the confidence to vocalise publicly will often confide to a microphone in both speech and song. There is an opportunity

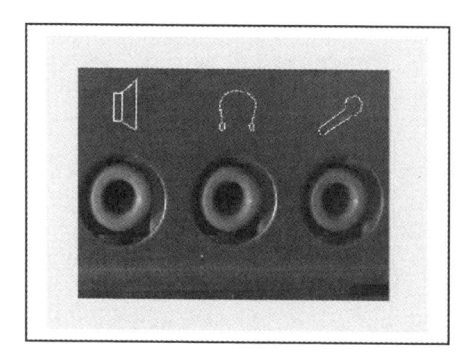

Figure 9.6 Icons indicating presence of a soundcard

here to meet some of the requirements from the curriculum to 'sing a few simple, familiar songs' and/or 'sing to themselves and make up simple songs' (QCA 2000)

Audio recording

A good program available on PCs is the Sound Recorder. It allows up to 60 seconds of recording and is as straightforward as an audio tape as it has standard start, stop and record buttons. Some children will already be familiar with these standard icons, as they are similar to remote controls for TV and video recorders. The beauty of Sound Recorder is that it is possible to play around with the recorded sounds – and create new and exciting sounds. These can be saved and then combined using the 'mix with file' option in the Edit drop down menu. Simply attach a microphone to your PC, then click on the circular record button to make a recording. Press stop once the recording is made, then press the 'stop' and 'play' buttons and your recording will play back from the beginning (see Figure 9.7).

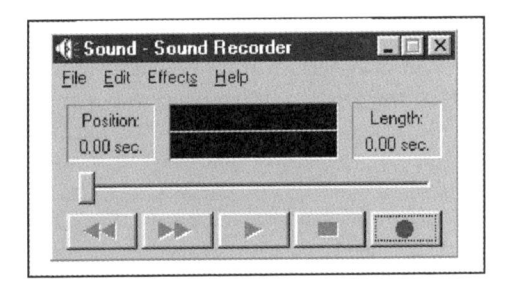

Figure 9.7 Sound Recorder: standard menu icons

Initially, the quality of recordings is likely to be poor, however, sound quality can be improved considerably. See 'Change the quality of a sound file' under 'Help' topics in Sound Recorder (see Figure 9.8).

Sampling

Sampling is the process of recording a sound then changing it. Use the Effects menu in Sound Recorder to change the speed, reverse it or add an echo. Try changing vocal, percussion or environmental sounds.

Further free advice can be found on the Internet on the LMP website under 'ICT for Free' (see: http://www.LMPi.co.uk/content/view/23/26/). There are further tips on using Sound Recorder on the BECTA (British Educational Communication and Technology Agency) ICT support site (see: http://www.becta.org.uk).

USING ICT TO ENHANCE THE LEARNING OF MUSIC   149

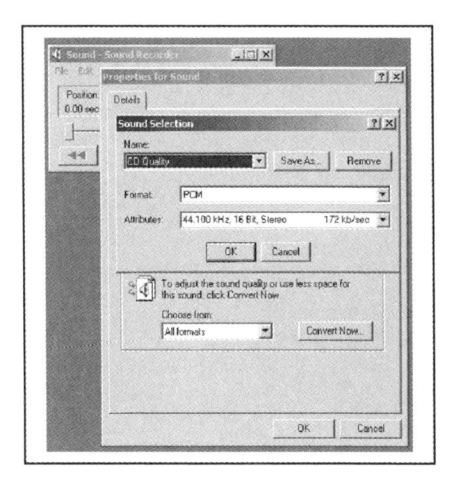

Figure 9.8 Sound Recorder: improving sound quality

CD, minidisk and MP3/MP4 portable recorders

These recorders in their portable formats make ideal recording tools for early years setting. The recordings are of a very high quality and sounds are stored as on a CD for quick search and playback. Environmental recordings are much clearer than with audio tape, and the recorders can be plugged into a computer to transfer the recordings. As with any new equipment, time is required to familiarise oneself with the instructions – but it is time well spent (see Figure 9.9).

Music keyboards

Children can use keyboards to explore sounds or to explore simple tunes. Pugh and Pugh (1998) suggest that they can be used to investigate timbre, pitch, tempo, dynamics and rhythm.

Adult support is very important as they can guide the children to explore alternative instruments and voices, 'transpose' options (which shifts the pitch of sounds higher or lower), altering the speed of a rhythm accompaniment, adjusting the volume control and selecting different rhythm accompaniment styles. One way of using a keyboard would be to use the sounds or effects of the keyboard to contribute to a sound picture or story. Some keyboards are specifically aimed at the early years and, although they might be classified as toys, they have useful applications in the early years setting.

Figure 9.9 A child holds a microphone to record sounds through a drainpipe while the teacher operates a portable minidisk recorder

Recording and playback: samplers

To 'sample' means to make a short recording which can then be used in various ways. Some keyboards, for instance, can record a sound (e.g. scrunching paper) and then this sound will be heard on all the keys – but at varying pitches. However, this aspect of keyboards is not now so readily available as it was 15–20 years ago. An alternative might be to record sounds using audio recording programs on computers then use the program's facilities to change the speed, pitch, quality, play it backwards and/ or add echo, etc.

Strategies for the use of technology

The use of information technology very often motivates children, but it requires careful planning to effectively integrate it with other activities. The use of technology is one area where support may well be needed. If the opportunity permits, a well briefed assistant, student or parent helper can assist the children. The technology should be planned to complement, support or enhance the teaching of music. For example, if the children are going to be working on patterns of sound, one group could create their pattern on a computer using a simple sequencer, another group could use percussion. In this way comparisons could be made between the different sound qualities of live and preset sounds, children's own sounds versus computer preset sounds and observations made regarding the immediacy of live performance versus recorded, such as, 'Is the technology a spur to live performance? And vice-versa?'

Some technological activities are best undertaken in pairs or small groups. Others, such as recording songs or changing sounds work well with larger groups. In such instances children can listen to and discuss improving or changing sounds.

Participation in making music, with the additional challenge of incorporating technology, can be seen as risk events – the children are making noise and are likely to get excited. Noise in music is similar to mess in painting. We tolerate it because it is worth it. Because music and music technology are creative subjects we rarely have an absolutely clear idea of the outcomes. For instance, we may decide to make a pattern of vocal sounds generated by the children, but not know what sounds they are going to invent. Likewise in painting, we may have patterns as a focus, but leave the child free to express their ideas within this given context. As the child grows in confidence and music becomes a normal everyday activity, noise and anxiety, and the courage to take risks, are rationalised.

Summary

This chapter has traced the development of technological developments that have made music more accessible to all. It argues for the experience of music including movement and language, in order to enhance aesthetic development. The work of Scarfe (1977), which relates musical progress to Bruner's (1973) stages of development, makes a plea for this experience to precede the use of notation. This is because research suggests that the introduction of technology initially, leads to an emphasis on that aspect of music education later. Four uses of ICT are explored in this chapter to develop the learning of music:

- awareness of the sound environment;
- responding to sound;
- categorizing sound by associating sounds with objects; and
- recording, playing and changing sounds.

There is a summary of technological aids, with an outline introduction to the types of software available. Finally, the chapter has included some useful advice for those who are new to the technologies.

References

Borland, J.E. (1927) A record of Musical Work in Schools and Training Colleges, *Musical Foundations*. Oxford: Oxford University Press.
Bruner, J.S. and Anglin, J.M. (1973) *Beyond the Information Given*. London: Allen and Unwin.
Kendell, I. (1977) The role of literacy in the school music curriculum, *Music Education Review*, 1.
Meadows, S. (1993) *The Child as Thinker*. London: Routledge.
Meer, W.V.D. (1980) *Hindustani Music in the 20th Century*. New Delhi: Allied Publishers Private.
Odam, G. (1995) *The Sounding Symbol*. Cheltenham: Stanley Thornes.
Paynter, J. (1982) *Music in the Secondary School Curriculum*. Cambridge: Cambridge University Press.
Pierson, A. (1987) *Compose Program Manual*. Nottingham: University of Nottingham.
Pierson, A. (1988) *Compose Program Manual*. Nottingham: University of Nottingham.
Pugh, A. and Pugh, L. (1998) *Music in the Early Years*. London: Routledge.
QCA (Qualifications and Curriculum Authority) (2000) *Curriculum Guidance for the Foundation Stage*, QCA/00/587. Sudbury: QCA Publications.
Rainbow, B. (1967) *The Land Without Music*. London: Novello.
Scarfe, J. (1977) Aesthetics and information technology. Unpublished MEd dissertation, University of Derby.
Tait, M. and Haach, P. (1984) *Principles and Processes of Music Education: New Perspectives*. New York: Columbia University.
Taylor, D. (1979) *Music Now*. Milton Keynes: Open University Press.
Van der Mear, W. (1980) *Hindustani Music in the 20th Century*. The Hague: Nijhoff NRC-Handelsbad.
Wiggins, T. (1978) *Conducting and Analysing Interviews*. Nottingham: University of Nottingham.
Wiggins, T. (1993) *Music of West Africa*. London: Heinemann Educational.

10

TOWARDS A FUTURE EARLY YEARS ICT CURRICULUM

Iram and John Siraj-Blatchford

Desktop computers have been around for a long time and in the rapidly changing high technology world, that we now find ourselves in, it is misleading to present them as 'new' technology. The first commercially successful Personal Computer (PC) was introduced a quarter of a century ago by IBM. It was in 1984 that Macintosh released the first mass-market computer to feature the (now ubiquitous) desktop graphic user interface (GUI) which presents files like pieces of paper that can be dragged and dropped into folders. Portable computers are now increasingly replacing the desktop units of the past, and dedicated hardware is increasingly being designed to integrate seamlessly into home and working environments. It is already becoming clear that the current keyboard, mouse and screen configurations will be replaced in the future by digital interfaces that utilise touch, gesture and voice controls.

In early childhood education the traditional distinction that has been made between technology education and educational technology are blurred and the educational implications of these developments are therefore profound. Given the rate of technological change it would be a mistake if practitioners were encouraged to emphasise PC operating skills as their most 'desired learning outcomes'. As Mitchell (2005) (among many) has recently argued:

> After almost a quarter of a century as the personal computing device of choice for business, the desktop PC is sliding off its pedestal. It has withstood assaults by technologies such as the Windows terminal, the Web and the network PC, but the mighty desktop has been humbled by user demand for the one thing it can't deliver – mobility
>
> (Mitchell 2005)

Creditably, the authors of this text have looked beyond the challenges of today's technology to consider learning objectives of more significance for the future lives of young children. Personal empowerment is the theme of the early chapters, and the emphasis on environmental citizenship, and 'teaching for tomorrow' by Mary Hayes (Chapter 1), Rosemary Feasey and Margaret Still (Chapter 5) are explicit. Similarly, Jackie Marsh (Chapter 8) argues that 'media literacy' has become increasingly important and that it has social, economic and political implications for the future.

Other chapters echo the concerns and priorities for developing *communication and collaboration, creativity, metacognition* and *learning to learn* that we have identified in our own research (Siraj-Blatchford and Siraj-Blatchford 2006). These are the attitudes, skills and understandings increasingly prioritised by developmental psychologists and early childhood educators, and they are also precisely those identified as being of special importance by politicians and economists in developing our future *knowledge society* (Siraj-Blatchford and Siraj-Blatchford 2006). This might be considered a very happy coincidence. In future knowledge societies, citizens will increasingly be required to control their own learning and critically evaluate and manipulate information in the development of new knowledge products. When we consider where it is in early years practice that such an agenda might be realised it is clear that socio-dramatic role-play offers special potential and Carol Fine and Mary Lou Thornbury's (Chapter 2) emphasis on the importance of play is therefore entirely appropriate. Given the importance of developing *communication and collaboration, creativity, metacognition* and *learning to learn*, each will be elaborated further in the following pages.

Communication and collaboration

There is general agreement among developmental psychologists and educationalists that collaboration is especially important in the early years. It is also within communicative and collaborative contexts that creativity and metacognition are developed in early childhood. When children share 'joint attention' or 'engage jointly' in activities we know that this provides a significant cognitive challenge in itself (Light and Butterworth 1992). Collaboration is also considered important in providing opportunities for cognitive conflict as efforts are made to reach consensus (Doise and Mugny 1984), and for the co-construction of potential solutions in the creative processes. But most unfortunately, as Crook (2003) has argued, and others have noted in the foregoing pages, designers have too often assumed that their task has been to develop software that support the learner in *solitary* acts of learning. What the designers have failed to recognise is the fact that the practices of private reflection and interrogation that are required to learn on one's own are at first developed through socially organised learning (Crook 2003). Also, while the value of ICT in supporting collaborative learning in schools has been demonstrated (Crook 1994), successful collaboration does not automatically occur simply whenever we bring children together to share the same computer. As Crook (1994) has shown, teachers often need to orchestrate collaborative interactions if there are to be learning gains. Crook also warns us that: '. . . while there is considerable evidence that ICT can be a powerful resource in helping to support joint working and classroom collaboration between school age pupils, it must be recognised that the social systems of pre-school environments have different dynamics' (Crook 2003: 13).

As David Whitebread (Chapter 6) suggests, computer-based adventure games and simulations have been found to be particularly powerful in generating collaborative talk and discussion. Programmable toys and many, if not most, other screen-based applications offer the possibility of collaboration in terms of symbolic manipulation, although adult intervention is often needed to gain the most from software. But as Tim Waller (Chapter 3) has noted, educators often underestimate children's experience and confidence with ICT. The UK *Effective Performance of Preschool Education* (EPPE) (Sylva et al. 1999), and *Researching Effective Pedagogy in Early Childhood* (REPEY) (Siraj-Blatchford et al. 2002) studies have shown that the most effective foundation stage settings combine the provision of free play opportunities with more focused group work involving adult direct instruction. This more balanced approach would therefore appear to be the most desirable model to promote with ICT as well.

The REPEY research also suggested that adult–child interactions that involved some element of 'sustained shared thinking' are especially valuable in terms of children's early learning. These were identified as sustained verbal interactions that moved forward in keeping with the child's interest and attention. They were initiations that were most commonly elicited in practical activity and they may often occur in the context of children's use of ICT. Unfortunately, the evidence also suggested that too often there is no adult present at these times to provide the necessary scaffolding and support (Siraj-Blatchford et al. 2002).

Creativity education and ICT in the early years

As Sawyer et al. (2003) argue, given the fact that the core insight of both Piaget and Vygotsky's constructivism was that children participate in the creation of their own knowledge, it is remarkable that so little connection has been made between creativity and child development by contemporary researchers.

As we have argued elsewhere, a good way to understand the development of young children's creativity may be to consider it in terms of the development and manipulation of 'schemes' (Siraj-Blatchford 2004). For Piaget (1969) and other developmental psychologists, a scheme is understood as an 'operational thought', it may be a recalled behaviour, the recollection of a single action or a sequence of actions. To be creative, children need to acquire a repertoire of schemes, and they also need the playful disposition to try out these schemes in new contexts. These trials may be expressed verbally, in the minds eye, or in the material world. Young children are naturally curious and they learn many of their schemes vicariously; they spontaneously imitate a wide range of the schemes provided by adults and other children. Vygotsky (2004) distinguished between two types of activity, those 'reproductive', and those involving 'combinations' or creativity: 'Creative activity, based on the ability of our brain to combine elements, is called imagination or fantasy in psychology' (2004: 4). In their fantasy play, young children quite naturally separate objects and actions from their meaning in the real world and give them new meanings. They should be encouraged to communicate these creative representations because it is in this way that their powers of expression and abstraction may be developed more generally (Van Oers 1999).

Educators may encourage the discovery of such schemes, and provide explicit models for the children to follow in their play. As Mary Hayes, Chris Taylor and David Wheway (Chapter 9) make clear in their chapter on early music education, all of this can be supported, and it *is* already regularly supported, by innovative early years practitioners using ICT. Both real and pretend ICTs may be integrated in support of socio-dramatic play, and this kind of play, is widely recognised to be of significant cognitive and socio-emotional benefit in its own right (Smalinsky 1990: 35). Computer applications such as Granada Learning's *At the Café* and *At the Vet's* allow children to imitate adult role behaviours, acting them out in their play and learning to understand them better. Pretend telephones, domestic equipment and point of sale technologies are employed to support children in their imitations and simulations of the adult world and human relationships through symbolic representation. Practitioners are also able to create supportive resources of their own using generic office tools such as word processors, paint and PowerPoint applications, and ICT has also been found to support creative socio-dramatic activity quite spontaneously. For example, Brooker and Siraj-Blatchford (2002) found that children often make little separation between the on-screen and the off-screen world: 'On-screen images were "grabbed", scolded, fingered and smacked, with dramatic effect, as part of the small-group interaction with the software. In some instances, they took on an off-screen life of their own, as children continued the game the computer had initiated, away from the machine' (2002: 267). Well designed on-screen applications provide for a wide variety of possible responses. As David Whitebread suggests in Chapter 6, adventure games and simulations often offer particular strengths. They also allow the child to try things out, and if they don't work, they can try something else.

Sylva et al. (1976) and Vandenberg (1980) have also shown that play facilitates problem-solving. Divergent thinking is central to both play and creativity, and longitudinal studies have also shown that creativity in pretend play is predictive of divergent thinking over time (Clark et al. 1989; Russ 2003). As Edwards and Hiler (1993) argued in their teacher's guide to Reggio Emilia, we should encourage young children in their day-to-day practices of analysis (e.g. seeing similarities and differences); synthesis (e.g. rearranging, reorganizing); and evaluation (e.g. judging the value of things).

Metacognition and learning to learn

As Richard Bennett suggests in Chapter 4, the notion that teachers should develop better ways of helping children learn how to learn was fundamental to Papert's (1980) constructionism and to the educational development of LOGO. In 2004, David Miliband, the UK Minister for School Standards, commissioned a report to clarify the concept of 'learning to learn'. The working group included leading academics and head teachers and in their final report they argued:

> [While] the more precise specification of the family of practices that constitute learning to learn must await both further psychological research and educational developments. We are for the present convinced that a very important or senior member of the family, one we regard as at the core of learning to learn, is metacognition ... Much of what teachers do in helping students to learn how to learn consists of strengthening their metacognitive capacity, namely the capacity to monitor, evaluate, control and change how they think and learn. This is a critical feature of personalised learning
>
> (Hargreaves 2005: 7, 18)

In Chapter 6 David Whitebread has argued that the ability to deal with higher order and more abstract relationships is dependent upon the use of language and other forms of symbolic representation. The implications of this for ICT education are identified further by Janet Cooke and John Woollard (Chapter 7) who describe projects in which children have been given specific play experiences to aid the development of symbolism. Cooke and Wollard cite research that shows that this supports the children's development of problem-solving and early literacy. Computers provide a means by which young children may be supported in their manipulation of symbols and representations on the screen in a useful manner that allows them to distance themselves from the signifying objects. Screen-based activities might therefore support the processes of verbal reflection and abstraction (Forman 1984). This is a theme specifically addressed by Bowman et al. (2001) in the US National Research Council's report *Eager to Learn: Educating our Preschoolers*. The report strongly endorses the application of computers in early childhood:

> Computers help even young children think about thinking, as early proponents suggested (Papert 1980). In one study, pre-schoolers who used computers scored higher on measures of metacognition (Fletcher-Flinn and Suddendorf 1996). They were more able to keep in mind a number of different mental states simultaneously and had more sophisticated theories of mind than those who did not use computers
> (Bowman et al. 2001: 229)

The *Concise Dictionary of Psychology* defines metacognition as: 'having knowledge or awareness of one's own cognitive processes' (Statt 1998). Metacognition has been associated with effective learning in numerous contexts (Larkin 2000), and the concept has also been applied by educators seeking to design effective pedagogy. There is a general consensus that metacognition develops as the individual finds it necessary to describe, explain and justify their thinking about different aspects of the world to others (Perner et al. 1994; Lewis et al. 1996; Pelligrini et al. 1997). For most children such a 'theory of mind' develops at about 4 years 6 months (Tan-Niam et al. 1999). Research shows that children's pretend play becomes reciprocal and complementary at about the same time (Howes and Matheson 1992). Research has established that a child with a 'theory of mind' is able to understand that other people have minds of their own; that other individuals have their own understandings and motivations; and that they usually act according to their individual understanding and motivations even when they are mistaken.

It can be seen from the above that those applications likely to be effective in supporting the development of metacognition are also those most effective in supporting socio-dramatic play. These are also the applications that tend to be more effective in supporting communication and collaboration.

As Katz and Chard (1996) have suggested perhaps the greatest contribution of Reggio Emilia to early childhood education is in their use of the 'documentation' of children's experience as a standard element in classroom practice. Documentation typically includes samples of a child's work at several different stages of completion; photographs show work in progress; comments are written by the teacher or other adults working with the children; transcriptions of children's discussions and comments; and explanations of intentions about the activity and comments made by the parents are recorded.

Documentation provides a means by which children are encouraged to reflect upon their own work and that of their peers. They therefore; 'become even more curious, interested, and confident as they contemplate the meaning of what they have achieved' (Malaguzzi 1993: 63). It provides a means by which the children's ideas and work may be validated. When the children's efforts, intentions, and ideas are shown so clearly to be taken seriously this encourages them to approach their work with greater responsibly, energy and commitment.

Documentation provides a means of communication with parents which may often lead to them to become more involved in their child's learning and may even lead to parents re-examining the assumptions that they have made regarding their own role in the child's education (Malaguzzi 1993: 64). Documentation also provides information for practitioner research and can serve to sharpen and focus the teachers' attention on the learning that is taking place within their setting.

Conclusions

Williams et al. (2004) make the case for robust futures thinking processes at local and national level and propose the concept of 'futures literacy' to describe the essential vocabulary, concepts and learning processes that we need to look beyond the horizon of conventional planning. In the context of creating an early childhood education appropriate to the development of our knowledge society; *communication and collaboration, creativity, metacognition* and *learning to learn*, provide the key constructs. As Crook (2003) and also Janet Cooke and John Woollard (Chapter 7) have argued, it is also important that practitioners become more closely engaged with hardware and software designers. If the full potential of ICT in early childhood education is to be realised children themselves must also be involved in these collaborative processes of technological design (Siraj-Blatchford 2004).

Technology moves on and this has profound implications for society, Papert (2001) provided a graphic illustration of this at a recent conference. As Papert (2001) observed, in the early 1940s and 1950s all the fastest ships crossing the Atlantic were European, and as the American's were embarrassed about that they decided to build the *SS United States* to be the fastest ship in the world (at a cost of US$79 million). The maiden voyage of the *SS United States* was on 3 July 1952. But unfortunately for them the British

Overseas Aircraft Corporation (BOAC) had inaugurated the world's first commercial jet airline service two months before that, on 2 May 1952. The service was provided by Sir Geoffrey De Havilland's 36-seater Comet (estimated cost £250,000). Overnight it became completely irrelevant which ship could travel across the Atlantic more quickly. As Papert argued, it is worth remembering this story when thinking about schools: 'Are we trying to perfect an obsolete system or are we trying to make the educational jet plane?' (Papert 2001: 112).

The pace of change in modern societies is particularly challenging for the school curriculum, which must respond (however indirectly) to these economic and cultural changes. As Carr (1998) has argued, the curriculum must be recognised as; 'a socially-constructed cultural artefact which (like society itself) has to be made and re-made in response to changing historical circumstances' (1998: 330).

From this perspective it is clear that the challenge for the early years is the most acute. While it is recognised that the need to prepare children with the knowledge and skills appropriate to their roles as future producers and consumers is only one of our educational priorities, it *is* a major priority, and it requires particularly careful foresight. The 3- and 4-year-olds of today will complete their statutory education in 2017 and 2018 and, given the exponential rate of technological development and advance that we are already experiencing, we can be sure that the economic and cultural realities at that time will be quite different to those experienced today. It is the context of these future contexts that decisions need to be made about the early years curriculum right now.

References

Bowman, B., Donovan, S. and Burns, S. (eds) (2001) *Eager to Learn: Educating our Preschoolers*. Washington, DC: Committee on Early Childhood Pedagogy, National Academic Press.

Brooker, E. and Siraj-Blatchford, J. (2002) 'Click on Miaow!': How children of three and four experience the nursery computer, *Contemporary Issues in Early Childhood*, 3(2).

Carr, W. (1998) The curriculum in and for a democratic society, *Curriculum Studies*, 6(3). Available at: http://www.triangle.co.uk/pdf/viewpdf.asp?j=cus&vol=6&issue=3&year=1998&article=wc&id=62.253.128.14 (accessed 11 March 2005).

Clark, P., Griffing, P. and Johnson, L. (1989) Symbolic play and ideation fluency as aspects of the evolving divergent cognitive style in young children, *Early Child Development and Care*, 51: 77–88.

Crook C. (1994) *Computers and the Collaborative Experience of Learning*. London: Routledge.

Crook, C. (2003) cited in Early learning in the knowledge society: Report on a European Conference, 22–3 May, Brussels. *International Business Machines* (IBM).

Doise, W. and Mugny, G. (1984) *The Social Development of the Intellect*. Oxford: Pergamon Press.

Edwards, C. and Hiler, C. (1993) *A Teacher's Guide to the Exhibit: The Hundred Languages of Children*. Lexington, KY: College of Human Environmental Sciences, University of Kentucky.

Fletcher-Flinn, C. and Suddendorf, T. (1996) Do computers affect the mind? *Journal of Educational Computing Research*, 15(2): 97–112.

Forman, E. (1984) The role of peer interaction in the social construction of mathematical knowledge, *International Journal of Educational Research*, 13: 55–69.

Hargreaves, D. (2005) *About Learning: Report of the Learning Working Group*. Available at: http://www.demos.co.uk//publications//aboutlearning

Howes, C. and Matheson, C.C. (1992) Sequences in the development of competent play with peers: Social and pretend play, *Developmental Psychology*, 28: 961–74.

Katz, L.G. and Chard, S.C. (1989) *Engaging Children's Minds: The Project Approach*. New Jersey: Ablex Publishing.

Katz, L.G. and Chard, S.C. (1996) The contribution of documentation to the quality of early childhood education, *ERIC Digest*, ED 393 608. Urbana, IL: ERIC Clearinghouse on Elementary and Early Childhood Education.

Larkin, S. (2000) How can we discern metacognition in year one children from interactions between students and teacher? Paper presented at ESRC Teaching and Learning Research Programme Conference, 9 November.

Lewis, C., Freeman, N.H., Kyriadicou, C., Maridaki-kassotaki, K. and Berridge, D. (1996) Social influences on false belief access: Specific sibling influences or general apprenticeship? *Child Development*, 67: 2930–47.

Light, P. and Butterworth, G. (eds) (1992) *Context and Cognition: Ways of Learning and Knowing*. Hemel Hempstead: Harvester Wheatsheaf.

Malaguzzi, L. (1993) History, ideas, and basic philosophy, in C. Edwards, L. Gandini and G. Forman (eds) *The Hundred Languages of Children: The Reggio Emilia Approach To Early Childhood Education*. New Jersey: Norwood.

Mitchell R. (2005) Decline of the desktop, *Computerworld*, 26 September. Available at: http://www.computerworld.com/hardwaretopics/hardware/story/0,10801, 104856,00.html

Papert, S. (1980) *Mindstorms: Children, Computers and Powerful Ideas*. New York: Basic Books.

Papert, S. (2001) Keynote address to the special forum on ICT and Education at the OECD on 2 April. Reproduced in full in OECD (2001) *Schooling for Tomorrow. Learning to Change: ICT in Schools*, Available at: http://www1.oecd.org/publications/e-book/9601131E.PDF (accessed 11 March 2005).

Pellegrini, A., Galda, L. and Flor, D. (1997) Relationships, individual differences and children's use of literate language, *British Journal of Educational Psychology*, (June), 67 (Pt. 2): 139–52.

Perner, J., Leekam, S.R. and Wimmer, H. (1994) Three-year-olds' difficulty with false belief, *British Journal of Developmental Psychology*, 5: 125–37.

Piaget, J. (1969) *The Mechanisms of Perception*. London: Rutledge & Kegan Paul.

Russ, S. (2003) Play and creativity: developmental issues, *Scandinavian Journal of Educational Research*, 47(3).

Sawyer, K., Moran, S., John-Steiner, V. et al. (2003) *Creativity and Development*. Oxford: Oxford University Press.

Sylva, K., Bruner, J.S. and Genova, P. (1976) The role of play in problem-solving of children 3–5 years old, in J.S. Bruner, A. Jolly and K. Sylva (eds) *Play: Its Role in Development and Evolution*. Harmondsworth: Penguin.

Sylva, K., Siraj-Blatchford, I., Melhuish, E. et al. (1999) *The Effective Provision of Pre-School Education (EPPE) Project: Technical Paper 6a. Characteristics of Pre-School Environments*. London: University of London/DfEE.

Siraj-Blatchford, J. (2004) *Developing New Technologies for Young Children*. Stoke on Trent: Trentham Books.

Siraj-Blatchford, I. and Siraj-Blatchford, J. (2006) *A Guide to Developing the ICT Curriculum for Early Childhood Education*. Stoke on Trent: Trentham Books in collaboration with Early Education (The British Association for Early Childhood Education).

Siraj-Blatchford, I., Sylva, K., Muttock, S. and Gilden, R. (2002) *Effective Pedagogy in the Early Years*. Research Report 356. London: DfES.

Smilansky, S. (1968) *The Effects of Sociodramatic Play on Disadvantaged Preschool Children*. New York: John Wiley and Sons.

Smilansky, S. (1990) Sociodramatic play: Its relevance to behavior and achievement in school, in E. Klugman and S. Smilansky (eds) *Children's Play and Learning*. New York: Teacher's College.

Statt, D.A. (1998) *The Concise Dictionary of Psychology*, 3rd edn. London: Routledge.

Sylva, K., Melhuish, E., Sammons, P., Siraj-Blatchford, I. and Taggart, B. (2004) *The Effective Provision of Pre-School Education (EPPE) Project: Technical Paper 12. The Final Report*. London: DfES/Institute of Education, University of London.

Tan-Niam, C.L.S., Wood, D.J. and O'Malley, C. (1999) Play initiation, reciprocity and theory of mind, *The Australian Journal of Research in Early Childhood Education*, 6(2): 73–83.

Van Oers, B. (1999) Teaching opportunities in play, in M. Hedegaard and J. Lompscher (eds) *Learning Activity and Development*. Aarhus: Aarhus University Press.

Vandenberg, B. (1980) Play, problem-solving, and creativity, *New Directions for Child Development*, 9: 49–68.

Vygotsky, L. (2004) Imagination and creativity in childhood, *Journal of Russian and East European Psychology*, 42(1): 4–84.

Williams, C., Horne, M., Mccarthy, H., Creasy, J. and Harris, S. (2004) Progress report on futuresight: England's contribution to the toolkit. London: Lead Country Papers. Presented at the OECD Forum on 'Schooling For Tomorrow' in Toronto, Canada.

INDEX

Abstract symbols: use of 31
Abstraction: ability to deal with 101–2
Abstraction process 56
Achievements: awareness of 15
Addition: ability by age of five 56
Adventure games 86, 157; characteristics of 87–90; decision making development 93–4; developing reasoning 93–4; early experiences 104; educational value of 96; fictional contexts 101; guidelines for use of 104; hypothesis testing with 93–4; information gathering and 90; interactive nature of 99; planning and strategies 91–3; problem solving skills and 92–3
Aesthetic development: music and 151
Affordances: understanding of 130
Age-specific teaching style 50
Alphabet: matching letters on computer 30
Amplification: sound 147
Amplifiers: music technology and 145
Analogy: learning by process of 97

Animation 25; film 125–7
Animation activity: skills gained in 132
Arithmetic 21
Artistic development 25–6
At the Cafe 156
At the Vet's 156
Audio recording 148; music technology and 146; sampling 148
Auditory literacy 28
Aural memory: ICT and 138–9
Awareness: of audience: understanding of 131; of difficulties and achievements 15

Bar charts 61
Beatles 137
Belgium: early years experience of children in 22
Bilingual learners: needs of 42–3
Black Cat Composer 142
Block graphs 61–2
Blogging 134
Blue Peter 3
Brush and colour bar 115

Brush size tool 115, 117

Cameras: use of 125
Capability: ICT 117–8
CD players 144
CD-ROM: cost of 29; design of 27–8; evaluation of 29; impact on children's reading 30; language development and 28; obtaining information from 12; potential of 34; reading development and 28; reading learning and 29; saving children's work to 133; use of for exploration and feedback 26–7
CDs 149
Challenges: children setting 99; setting level of 98
Change: pace of in modern society 160
Child development: relationship with creativity 156
Children: as learners 18; development of 100
Classifying 61
Classroom practice: implications of software 121
Cognitive processes: awareness of 158; monitoring and evaluating 102
Cognitive-motor skills: difficulties in learning complex 18
Collaboration 154–5, 159
Collaborative learning 102, 155
Collaborative writing 48
Colour: use of 25
Communication 159; importance of 154–5; in science 77–8
Communication technology: development and use of 43–5
Communicative practices 44
Compose Junior 142
Compose World Junior 142
Composition: music 138
Computer based activity: frequency of 66
Computer games: element of chance in 13; progress with reference to 15; role of in supporting learning 40–1
Computer programs *see* Software
Computer suites: advantages of 68; timetabling 24
Computers: advantages of using with children 22; children's knowledge of 9–11; children's knowledge of how affect peoples' lives 14–5; children's learning about at home 16; children's perceptions of access to 11; confidence of young children in use of 14; engagement with 33; feedback provided by 99; freedom to make mistakes using 93; importance of operating skills 153; knowledge considered when children use 7–8; knowledge embodied in 8; location of children's learning about 14; loss of creativity by using 25; opportunities to gain confidence in use of 18; promoting literacy 28; rules for children's use at home 11; scepticism over benefits in early years education 39–40; social references to 15; use of in nursery school 45–6; used by young children 6; using to access material 9
Confidence: opportunities to gain in use of computers 18
Contingency mobile experiment 99
Control strategies: development of 102–3
Counting: matching numbers on computer 30
Creative process: learning and 96–9
Creativity 154, 159; development of 25; ICT and 107–8; ICT in developing 86; loss of by using computers 25; relationship with child development 156
Critical skills: development of 132
Cultural tools: acquisition of 3
Culture: communicators of 21
Curriculum 4; literacy 38; need to maintain appropriate literacy 42; need to redefine in respect of literacy 37, 43; prescribed by Government 39
Customization: software should allow 120

Dance mats 144
Data collection: automatic 76
Data handling 61–3; successful use of software 63–4
Databases: advantages of 63; drawback of some 62–3

INDEX

Decision making: adventure games developing 93–4
Developmental psychology 6
Digital cameras: use of in science 81–3
Digital communications: proliferation of 134
Digital film production 124–7; relationship between ICT and 125
Digital photographs: of children's activities sent home 43
Digital tape recording 137
Digital technology: development of 37; impact of 41; potential of 38
Digital toys: potential of 41–2; to assist literacy 41
Documentation: children's experiences 159
Drill: aspect of programmed learning 58; software 65, 67

E-learning: move away from to m-learning 38
E-mail 2
Eager to Learn: Educating our Preschoolers 158
Editing: film 125–6
Effective Performance of Preschool Education 155
Effective questioning 77
Electric guitar: introduction of 137
Electric organ: development of 137
Electronic instruments: based on oscillators 137
Electronic literacy 4, 44
Electronic media: children's perspective of 41
Electronic toys: used by young children 6
Emergent mathematics 56
Emergent writing 56
Environmental citizenship 154
Evaluation: cognitive processes 102
Experimentation: learning by 120

Feedback: from computer 99
Fictional contexts: adventure games 101
Fill function 117
Fill tool 115
Film production: early years 132–3
Finding Nemo 131

'Forgiveness': in user interface 118–9

Gender: identity in technology 27
Genre: understanding of 132
Geometry: extension into area of 31
Globalization 3–4
Gramophone: invention of 136
Granada Learning 156
Granny's Garden 104
Graphic user interface 57, 153
Graphics 25, 44
Graphing packages 61
Groupwork 102

Headphones: music technology and 146
Headstart program 23
Holistic development: child's disposition to learn 22
Human computer interface: importance of in ICT 108
Human rights 2
Hungary: early years experience of children in 22
Hypertext 44
Hypothesis testing: adventure games developing 93–4

Icons 110–1; children's understanding of 112-4; function of 118; need for standardization of 119–20; recognition of 114–5; use of 24
Identity: development of 3
Immaturity: nature and uses of 97
iMovie2 126, 129–31
Impact Project 63
Impulsivity-reflectivity: memory tasks 100
Individualised learning 102
Induction: learning by process of 97
Infant learning: factors in 21
Information: gathering 77, 90–1; handling and using 3; management 3, 12, 90–1; processing 100–1
Information and Communications Technology (ICT): applications in science 79–81; capability 117–8; continuing potential of 159; contribution to early years science 76–7; creativity and 107–8; early

literacy and 37–50; effect on children's learning 41; effective pedagogies using 24; freedom offered by 98; help in learning to read 46–7; impact on children's achievement 63; importance of human computer interface 107–8; improving aural memory 138–9; in developing creativity 86; in development of written language 45; influence on literacy 39; instant feedback from science and 78–9; investment in 38; justification in early literacy activities 40; lack of joint activity in 49; music teaching and 136–9; networked 43; promotion of literacy by 39; relationship between digital film production and 125; relationship between science and 72–85; research into use of 40–50; role of teacher changes as result of introduction into classroom 50; role of teacher in learning with 50–1; software used by teachers 64–8; special tools offered by 76–7; statutory requirement to use 64; supporting early literacy 48–9; transferable skills in use of 45; types of learning involved 17; understanding of 8; use of in New Zealand to support literacy in English and Maori 43; use with reception class children 67

Information technology (IT): strategies of use in teaching music 150–1; understanding of 8

Input devices: problems in relation to 12

Instructions: ability to give 32

Intel Play QXA Computer Microscope 81, 83–5

Interface design 111

Interface metaphors 110

Internet 2, 43; growth of 3; obtaining information from 12

Joystick: difficulties in using 12

Jungle Book 131

Karaoke machines 147

Keyboard: use of compared to writing 13

Knowledge: computers opening door to new 18; developed in animation activity 127; different types of 8; slow consolidation of 22; used as a commodity 3

Knowledge society: development of 159

Language: CD-ROM and development 28; development of 97; in problem solving 102; in scaffolding 102; science in 79–80; social interaction and 102; use of precise 32

Learning: children's preferred mode of 12; developments in 96–9; psychology of 96–9; types of involved in ICT 17

Learning dispositions: science 74–5

Learning to learn 154, 159

Literacy: changing nature of 39; complexity of early years 39; computer for promoting 28; computers promoting 28; cultural mismatch between home and school experiences 42; curriculum 38; digital toys to assist 41; exploitation of new technology to advance definition of 44; ICT and early 37–50; ICT supporting early 48–9; ICT to promote 39; influence of ICT on 39; integration of instruction and technology 47; justification for use of ICT in activities 40; need to maintain appropriate curriculum 42; need to redefine understanding of curriculum 43; range of 44

Logical thinking 32

LOGO 58–60; preparatory activities for 60–1

Loop-based programs: music 142

M-learning: move away from e-learning to 38

Making Tracks: Radio 3's website for children 143

Maori: use of ICT in New Zealand to support literacy in English and 43

Mathematical knowledge: implicit 56

Mathematics 15; computer games for early learning 30; current thinking on teaching of 55–7; programmable robots as aid to 31–3; software 58; software

used in 64–8; teaching methods 57; use of LOGO in teaching 58–60
Measurement 32
Media: learning through wide range of 44
Media education: lack of in early years 123–4; place of in early years education 124–6; scope of 124
Media literacy: Government emphasis on 133–4; importance of 154
Memory tasks 100
Metacognition 154, 157; definition of 158
Metacomponents 102–3
Metamemory: memory tasks 100
Metaphors: interface 110; need for standardization of 119–20; use of 109
Microphones: music technology and 144
Minidisks 149
Mistake: correcting with 'undo' button 116–7
Mobile phones 134
Moblogging 124
Monitoring: cognitive processes 102
Moog synthesiser 137
Moon landing 1
Motor skills: using mouse 26
Mouse: development of motor skills 26; difficulties in using 12; experimentation with 24; physical skills with 15
Mouse menu button 117
MP3/MP4 portable recorders 144, 149
Multilingual learners: needs of 42–3
Multimedia 38
Multimodality: understanding of 129
Multitrack recording 137
Music: composition 138; ICT and teaching of 136–9; loop-based programs 142; software supporting teaching of 141; strategies for use of IT in teaching of 150–1; teaching methods 138; understanding quality of 140
Music keyboards 144, 149
Music technology: for early years teaching 143–4
Music Toolkit 142
Musical appreciation 138

Narrative: understanding of 128–9
National Literacy Strategy 50
National Numeracy Strategy 56
National Research Council (US) 158
Neuronal networks 97
New Zealand: use of ICT to support literacy in English and Maori 43
Numerals: recognition of 32; universality of 33
Nursery children: use of computers by 24
Nursery school: use of computers in 45–6

Office for Communications (Ofcom) 133–4
Ondes Martenot: invention of 137
Open-ended tools: use of 30
Operational thought 156
Opportunities: to gain confidence in use of computers 18
Oscillators: electronic instruments based on 137
Outcome goals: shift from process goals to 18

Paint programs: artistic development and 25; children's use of 112–4; experimentation using 24–5; use of 22–3; importance of 121
Performance: memory tasks 100
Personal computers: introduction of 153
Phonograph: sound recording on 137
Piaget, Jean [1896–1980] 96
Piagetian theory 59
Pictograms 61
Pictures: enforcement of stereotypes by 25
Pitch: differentiating extremes of 140
Planning: adventure games developing 91–3
Plasticity 103
Play: as learning medium 98; facilitating problem solving 157; impact of technology on 41; nature and purpose of 97; repetitive 99; role of ICT in supporting 40; significance of 34
Play situations 16
Portable computers 153
Powered speakers: music technology and 146

PowerPoint applications 156
Practice: aspect of programmed learning 58; software 65, 67
Printing 116
Problem solving 87–90, 92–3; children's approach to 12; development of 158; language in 102; play facilitating 157; tools for 94–6; use of ICT to develop 2
Process goals: shift from to outcome goals 18
Programmed learning 58
Programming: early stages of 32
Programs *see* Software
Progress: expression of 16; reference to computer games 15
Pupil agency 6

Questioning: effective 77
Questions: encouraging children to frame 12

Radio 3: website for children 143
Radio: invention of 136
Reading 15, 21; CD-ROM in development 28; ICT help in learning 46–7; overemphasis on formal skill of 43; use of talking books 46–7
Reading difficulties 15
Reasoning: adventure games developing 93–4; context dependent 101
Reception children 24
Recorded music: editing 137
Recorders: music technology and 144–5
Representational material 22
Research: into use of ICT 37–50
Researching Effective Pedagogy in Early Childhood (REPEY) 155
Rhythm: play with 140
Rhythm machines 142–3
Robot command: grammar of 32
Robots: programmable as aid to mathematics 31–3

Sampling: audio recording 148, 150
Scaffolding 62; language and 102
Science: as social activity 78; communication in 77–8; digital cameras in 81–3; ICT applications in 79–81; ICT contribution to early years 76–7; instant feedback using ICT 78–9; language in 79–80; learning dispositions 74–5; relationship between ICT and 72–85; use of sensors in 80–1
Scientific investigation 77
Screen display 25
Self-regulation: developmental phases in 18
Sensors: use of in science 80–1
Sequencing: commands 32; software for 141–2
Simulated problems: designing 88
Simulations 157; characteristics of 87–90; educational value of 96; guidelines for use of 104
Skills: developed in animation activity 127
Social activity: science as 78
Social interaction: language and 102
Social isolation: fears of 40
Social learning 32
Social tools: acquisition of 3
Socialisation: children into school 11–2
Socio-dramatic play 158
Software 22; conceptual structure of 16; data handling 61–3; drill 65, 67; evaluation of 64; for sequencing 141–2; frequency of use 66; implications for classroom practice 121; importance of design 34; lack of understanding about structure of 13; mathematics 58; messages in 4; practice 65, 67; problems of open-ended 60; quality of 27–8, 67; selection of 68–9; should allow customization 120; simulation 90–1; successful use of data handling 63–4; supporting music teaching 141; used by teachers in conjunction with ICT 64–8
Sorting 61
Sound 25, 44; amplification 147; categorizing and associating 140–1; responding to 140; use of 25
Sound environment: awareness of 139
Sound processing 147–8
Sound Recorder: on PCs 148
Sound recording 136–7
Soundcards: music technology and 146–7

INDEX

Space 32
Space exploration 1–2
Spatial awareness 32
Speakers: music technology and 145–6
Special educational needs 65
Speech feedback facility: desirability of 50
Spray tool 114–5, 117
Standardization: need for of metaphors and icons 119–20
Stereotyping: in CD-ROMS 27
Strategies: adventure games developing 91–3
Strategy use: memory tasks 100
Subtraction: ability by age of five 56
Super-Duper-Music-Looper 142
Sustained shared thinking 155
Symbolic distancing 109
Symbolism 108–9
Symbols: introduction of 28

Talking books 38; advantages of 29; in learning to read 46–7
Talking word processors 38
Tape recorders 144
Tape recording: digital 137
Teachers: awareness of children as learners 18; role of in learning with ICT 50–1; training of in use of technology 38
Teaching: constructivist approach to 61
Teaching for tomorrow: concept of 1
Teaching methods: mathematics 57
Technological change: pace of 38
Technology: development of 1–2; exploitation of to advance definition of literacy 44; for early years music teaching 143–4; integration of instruction and in literacy development 47; male gender identity universal in 27; socio-economic background determining access to new 39; speed of development 41, 159–60; training of teachers in use of 38
Television 1; children's response to 3
Terminology: children's use of 11
Text function 117–9
Theremin 137
Thinking: rationale behind children's 15; use of ICT to develop 2
Time-space compression 2
Tools: communicating 22
Toy Story 2 131
Transfer: issue in learning 101
Transmission techniques 22
Trial and error: learning by 120
Turtle graphics 59; LOGO 60–1
2Beat 142
2Explore 142
2Simple 142

Understanding: developed in animation activity 127–8
'Undo' button 116–7
'Undo' function 117, 119
United Nations Organisation 2
User interface: 'forgiveness' in 118–9; young children's use of 119–21

Video 44
Visual literacy 28
Visual recognition 117–8
Visual skills: development of 128
Vocabulary: introduction of 27

Whole child learning 16
Word processing 13, 116
Word processors: advantage of 47–8
World Health Organisation 2
World Wide Web 19; false assumptions about 39
Writing 21; collaborative 48; overemphasis on formal skill of 43
Written language: use of ICT in development of 45

Related books from Open University Press
Purchase from www.openup.co.uk or order through your local bookseller

SUPPORTING ICT IN THE EARLY YEARS
John Siraj-Blatchford and David Whitebread

Supporting ICT in the Early Years helps readers understand how very young children (from birth to six) develop an early awareness, and subsequently develop their knowledge, skills and understandings of information and communication technologies (ICTs).

The rapid growth of ICT has prompted concerns among parents, educators and policy-makers over the suitability of many educational applications, and electronic toys, for young children. However, evidence is presented to show that the use of ICT by young children is compatible with the principles of a developmentally appropriate curriculum (DAC). In fact the authors argue that used imaginatively, many applications of ICT can make a significant and unique contribution to children's social and cognitive development.

This is a significant book for parents, carers, teachers and other professionals who want to provide a rich learning environment in this area of experience.

Contents
An integrated approach to ICT education – ICT in the home, the local environment and early years education – Responding to the differing needs of children – Programmable toys, turtles and control technology – Painting, drawing and constructing images – Stories, narratives, simulated environments and adventure games – The Internet, websites and communications – Conclusions: the way forward – Appendices – References – Index.

128pp   0 335 20942 4 (Paperback)   0 335 20943 2 (Hardback)

PROMOTING CHILDREN'S LEARNING FROM BIRTH TO FIVE
SECOND EDITION

Angela Anning and Anne Edwards

Review of the first edition:
> Innovative, resourceful and thoroughly researched ... a challenge to existing and emerging early childhood professionals.
>
> *Contemporary Issues in Early Childhood*

Promoting Children's Learning from Birth to Five supports early years professionals as they develop new practices to promote young children's learning. This second edition fully reflects the enormous changes in early childhood education and care since the publication of the first edition. Retaining its successful focus on literacy and mathematical development as key exemplars of promoting young children's learning, the book considers new ways of working with parents, promoting inter-professional collaboration, and achieving sustainable, systematic change in children's services.

The second edition:

- Draws on current research in early literacy and mathematical thinking
- Focuses on multiprofessional practice, showing how practitioners who work from evidence across professional boundaries are able to give strong, interactive and sensitive support to young children and their parents
- Takes into account policies and practices such as Every Child Matters, the Primary Strategy and Children's Centres
- Includes updated material on aspects of leadership, and on the role of the Senior Practitioner in developing innovative services for children and their families
- Explores the importance of personal, social and emotional development in the curriculum for under-fives

Working from the basis that children learn most readily in contexts where parents and professionals are keen to learn, the authors help early childhood professionals to meet the challenges of reshaping children's services.

This is key reading for all early childhood professionals and students.

Contents

Introduction – Setting the national scene – The integration of early childhood services – The inquiring professional – Young children as learners – Language and literacy learning – How adults support children's literacy learning – Mathematical learning – How adults support children's mathematical learning – Creating contexts for professional development in educare – Early childhood services in the new millennium

Mar 2006   224pp   0 335 21970 5 (Paperback)

THE EXCELLENCE OF PLAY
SECOND EDITION

Janet Moyles (ed)

The second edition of this bestselling book encapsulates all the many changes that have taken place in early childhood in the last ten years. Whilst retaining its original message of the vital importance of play as a tool for learning and teaching for children and practitioners, it consolidates this further with current evidence from research and practice and links the most effective practice with the implementation of recent policies.

New contributions for the second edition include:

- Children as social and active agents in their own play
- Practitioners' roles in play and adults' enabling of play
- Play and links with Foundation Stage and FS Profile/legislation and policy
- KS1 links (and beyond)
- Birth to three matters
- Outdoor and physical play, including rough and tumble
- Gender differences
- Play and observation/assessment
- Special Educational Needs and play
- Parents' perspectives on play
- Child development links and play

The importance of curriculum and assessment is retained and extended. *The Excellence of Play* supports all those who work in early childhood education and care in developing and implementing the highest quality play experiences for children from birth to middle childhood. All the contributors are experts in their fields and all are passionate about the excellence of play. The book will stimulate and inform the ongoing debate about play through its powerful – and ongoing argument – that 'a curriculum which sanctions and utilizes play is more likely to provide well-balanced citizens of the future as well as happier and more learned children in the present'.

Contributors

Lesley Abbott, Ann Langston, Sian Adams, Angela Anning, Pat Broadhead, Tina Bruce, Tricia David, Sacha Powell, Bernadette Duffy, Hilary Fabian, Aline-Wendy Dunlop, Rose Griffiths, Nigel Hall, Stephanie Harding, Jane Hislama, Alan Howe, Dan Davies, Neil Kitson, Theodora Papatheodorou, Linda Pound, Peter Smith, David Whitebread, Helen Jameson.

Contents

Introduction – Play and curriculum – Birth to three matters and play – Supporting creativity/identity – Play and SENPlay, language and gender – Impact of play on storytelling – Play, literacy and the teacher – Role play – Outdoor play – Physical and rough and tumble play – Play and Science/Technology – Playing Music – Art in the early years – Mathematics and Play – Play in transitions – Play and different cultures – Reflecting on PlayPlay, the universe and everything – Afterword

c.288pp   0 335 21757 5 (Paperback)   0 335 21758 3 (Hardback)

Open up your options

- Education
- Health & Social Welfare
- Management
- Media, Film & Culture
- Psychology & Counselling
- Sociology
- Study Skills

for more information on our publications visit **www.openup.co.uk**

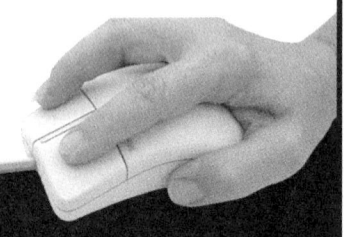

OPEN UNIVERSITY PRESS
McGraw · Hill Education